The Business of Marriage

The Business of Marriage

Management Techniques
For Your Most Important Partnership

Melissa Thoma

MelissaT@ThomaThoma.com
www.melissathoma.com

ISBNs: 978-1-7346901-1-8 (hardcover)
978-1-7346901-2-5 (paperback)

Copy editing: Liz Russell
Illustrations: Jade Pfeifer
Front cover design: Rachel Byrd
Author photos: Nancy Nolan
Book design: H. K. Stewart

Several chapters in this book were originally published on womenentrepreneur.com and are reprinted here with permission.

Printed in the United States of America

For **Martin,**
my partner in business and life.

And for **Claire** and **Sam,**
who endured more than their share
of business discussions over family dinner.

With love to you all!

Contents

Production and Operations/Resource Management

Leadership and Human Resources

Strategic Planning

In this Together, For Better or Worse

Good business practices translate well to marriage—in itself a decidedly risky business.

We were the typical starry-eyed lovers: young (our parents would say too young), full of potential, open to any possibility— with the super-charged hormones of nineteen-year-olds. We had fresh college degrees and were ready to leave our mark on the real world. And we had each other. Nothing could stop us. Right?

After several decades of marriage, we look back and have to laugh. Real life has not only shaped us at times but has slapped us around a bit, too. Learning to live together, learning to work together, learning to parent and to manage together through poverty and prosperity has been much more like a roller-coaster ride than the glorious ascent to fame, fortune, and romantic rapture we envisioned when we embarked on our shared life.

What my husband, Martin, and I have after all these years is a partnership: solid, secure, rewarding. Six years into marriage we went into business together, creating a marketing firm with $700 and a first-generation Apple Macintosh computer, using our back bedroom as an office. We discovered something in the process: our best business practices have turned out to be some of the best practices for our marriage.

What about your joint venture? You've pledged your life to your partner in the name of love and passion. You may have set a wedding date, decided to move in together, or just celebrated an anniversary. Let me ask you a few key questions: Would you sign the paperwork on a new business partnership without first creating a business plan? Would you put out the OPEN sign without setting up a budget or clearly defining job responsibilities? How long do you think your business would last if one of you dreamed of becoming the next Sam Walton, and the other wanted to create an exclusive boutique?

You've committed your life to your significant other, but have you created a life plan together? Martin and I have observed that most couples don't stop the business of life long enough to plan that business. And that's a real shame, because while new businesses fail at a surprising rate, new marriages fail at an even higher one. Using our business plan as a model, Martin and I have been life planning for years, and we believe it has made a big difference.

When we work with clients, Martin and I begin every planning consultation by posing the same question: what does your business look like five years from now? We then push our clients to create a vivid picture of the future, detailing accomplishments, changes, dollars—even the physical environment and relationships. Sometimes, as we seek honest assessments, the picture doesn't seem too rosy. "If we don't make a change, we won't be here in five years," some clients say.

We find this exercise very enlightening because the demands of running the business often prevent our clients from stepping back to define or refine their goals.

When was the last time you answered this question in your personal life? Have you sat down with your life partner and painted a detailed picture of your next five years together? Where will you live? Will one of you have a new job? Are there kids in the picture? If you maintain the present course, will you be happy five years from now? Begin with this conversation.

This book will work through the business of planning and managing your life using the same tools most businesses use to operate successfully. We're talking about everything from budgets to organizational charts. Engaging in a meaningful conversation about these issues can create clarity and an environment for productive negotiation, something every relationship can use.

Each morning when I come into work, I get my coffee, switch on my computer, and seat myself right beside my husband, who is sitting not five feet from my terminal. I'm reminded again: we are in this together … for better or worse. You are, too. And you can partner for a Fortune 500 success or a Chapter 11 reality check. Putting a little business into your relationship might be the difference.

Marriage is a Merger, Not an Acquisition

Like companies combining cultures,
couples need to plot out their merger.

Acquisition: [noun] The act of acquiring or gaining a possession
Merger: [noun] The combination of entities from two to one

*W*hich is marriage, "merger" or "acquisition"? It seems like a simple question with an obvious answer. We don't "acquire" a spouse; we "merge" as a couple. "Two become one," as the mantra goes.

As I reflect on the Business of Marriage, however, I'm not so sure our typical expectations really align with that cut-and-dried answer. Half of marriages fail. Could the M&A question have anything to do with that? Can business teach us any useful relationship lessons? I believe it can.

Acquiring a business is a relatively straightforward way to grow an enterprise, diversify your offerings, or even become an entrepreneur in the first place. The objective is quite simple: to gain possession of the business and its assets—people, processes, equipment, and revenue streams. Once you acquire, you control; its future, its culture, its operations are yours to decide. You've added an important asset to your balance sheet. The future is exciting.

I recall the early years of marriage. My desire to be married and my understanding of what a marriage would bring were, should I say, acquisitive. All I could think of was "getting my man!" Oh, the bounty of love and romance that would be mine as a married woman. A big warm toaster oven in bed every night. Kisses each morning. I could have a baby if I wanted. I would have someone to spend the rest of my life with! I don't recall spending much time thinking about the reality of a "merged" life with Martin.

In business, mergers are easily understood in theory—and devilishly hard to achieve in reality. Some say mergers have only about a thirty percent success rate. And it makes sense. In a merger, no one entity gets to dominate the equation. A new business is being created from the two that preceded it. What happens to the old systems, processes, and cultures of the two previous businesses? New ones have to be constructed, blending the highest and best of each single entity into some sort of new and agreed-upon design.

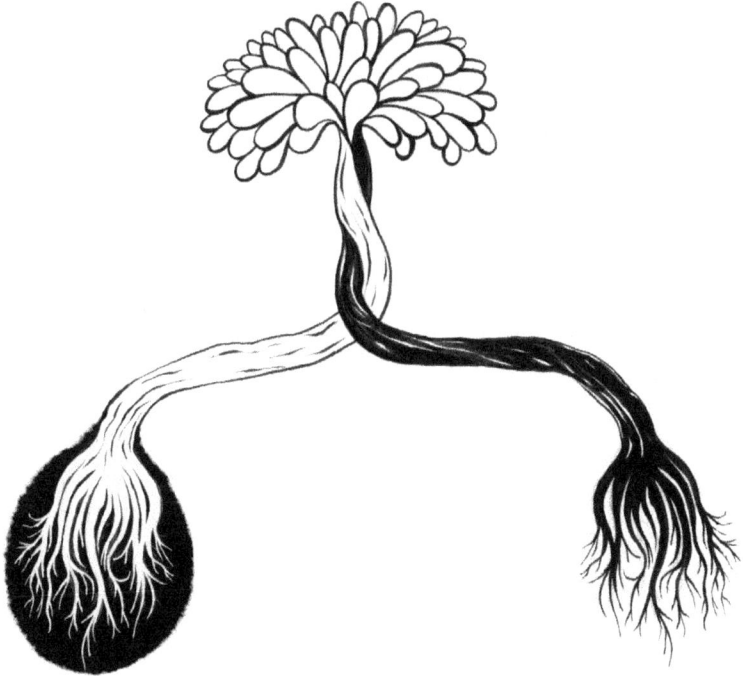

Some of this work is natural and organic; much is intentional and negotiated. Sounds like a marriage, doesn't it?

So how do you "merge" successfully? You have to understand that operating as a unit looks entirely different from operating as two individual entities. Companies that succeed with mergers follow a few fundamentals.

Establish the cultural mores, values, and principles that will govern the joined business.

Just like companies, people come to their unions with all their own "stuff." Successful companies sort this stuff out going into the deal. Couples can, too.

What must change for the sake of the merger? To be successful together, Martin and I agreed to give up yelling, something that was a fairly regular occurrence in my family but didn't sit well with Martin. We also determined not to spank our children. This would be better for us, even if it demanded more patience and more creative ways of dealing with the kids.

Something may work fine for *me*, but how should *we* do it? Think of the opportunity a merger presents to create a culture that is truly supportive of the marriage—and not just the individuals within it. That may mean sharing more financially than you might otherwise, or realigning how the household is run. As Tim Gunn, host of *Project Runway*, wisely advises, "Make it work!"

Parenting is an area that can stir up all kinds of conflict as couples attempt to face the challenge. If the two of you were raised very differently, it stands to reason that trying to create a united front and parent effectively can be challenging.

Develop an integration plan.

Slow down. Merging companies takes time, thought, and real communication. This is great advice for any couple considering a lifetime merger. Acknowledge the redundancies and make a plan for how you will deal with them. Don't let the changes take you by surprise or anger you. They're inevitable. Companies are really smart about this, and generating "economies of scale" is often a primary driver for merging in the first place. Couples, on the other hand, are more likely just to fight about it.

Identify the boundaries between "me" and "we." This is one of the most important areas to work on consciously. Think about it this way. If you're a Suburban and he's a coupe, are you going to be a new-fangled crossover? Or will you agree to merge onto the highway of life together and maintain your separate identities? Understanding what marriage means in terms of your identity is a crucial discussion you need to have. How much freedom will you agree to give one another? What is "too merged"?

For many couples the line between interdependence and co-dependence is blurry. Businesses merging have to determine the appropriate roles that leadership will assume within the newly merged companies as well. Some of our clients who have success-fully merged do so with both leadership teams basically intact, running as fairly separate entities yet sharing resources and taking advantage of those aforementioned economies of scale. I've seen successful marriages that operate on the same princi-ples. The couple cohabitates but vacations, socializes and develops their personal careers very much separately. Martin and I have a much more cohesive and merged marriage, but some-times we recognize we have to give each other some space in order to maintain our separate identities. This is an important conversation and it requires that you are both willing to step back and analyze your relationship from time to time in order to adjust.

Deploy a strong internal communications program.

Successful business mergers have great internal communications programs that keep employees apprised of what's happening, when, and why. We all know the importance of communications to a great relationship. Consider adding an intentionally designed program of communication around the question, "How's our merger doing?" Useful topics can be: "Is our merger producing the desired results?" "How is 'employee morale'?" "Are the 'corporate cultures' integrating or creating power struggles?" You can probably think of others.

Allocate resources intentionally.

Businesses and marriages have finite resources—living space, time, money, "stuff," holidays, and vacation days. A lot of things can be sorted consciously:

- **Households:** Where do we live? What do we keep, and what do we trash? Whose bed stays? Whose beloved great aunt's china do we keep? Don't even think about the Barcalounger.

- **Holidays:** Whose traditions are honored? With whom do we spend the holidays and where?

- **Finances:** The free credit report guy is right: it pays to know your partner's credit score. How will we set up our bank accounts?

- **Household duties:** This is where a guy can sometimes mistake merger for acquisition, believing he is gaining a cook and bottle-washer. And gals can often shake off all responsibility for car, lawn and home maintenance when in fact there are no real gender biases around any of these roles, so talk it out!

- **Time:** It's priceless and no longer all yours … it's a shared resource to be bargained for and jointly managed.

Merging businesses understand that resource allocations should be designed for the good of the whole, not for one or the other of the merging entities. Couples don't necessarily adopt this attitude.

Are you tired yet? Marriage, like business, is hard work. All the happiness, contentment, and self-realization produced by a high-performance relationship isn't something you *get*. It's something you *create* from giving and receiving support, love, and care. From two individuals, the merger creates a family: an organizational model that supports growth, change, stability, and self- discovery.

That's not a bad asset to have on life's balance sheet.

Business Pitfalls are Marriage Pitfalls

Avoiding both enhances your chances
of success—at home and the office.

*I*n all my years in business, I've never seen anything like the 2008–2011 economic crisis. To call it challenging is a gross understatement. Thousands of businesses and millions of jobs went under as a result of this economic tsunami, washed away under the extreme pressure from outside.

It made me think of dear friends who lost fundamentally solid relationships due to the pressure of events outside their control: the loss of a child, a devastating illness, or a family crisis. Businesses and relationships can fail under these extreme circumstances.

But what about the not-so-extreme circumstances? What are some of the foundational keys to success that, when they go missing, can undermine an otherwise successful business? What can we learn from business dangers that can help us in marriage?

In an article in *Business Know-How*, staff writer Patricia Shaefer lists some reasons for business failures. I'd like to re-examine her points in light of marriage ("The Seven Pitfalls of Business Failure and How to Avoid Them," *Business Know-How*, www.business-knowhow.com, 2011).

Point No. 1: Maybe you started your business for the wrong reasons.

Whenever I talk to folks about starting a business, I tell them the three golden rules of entrepreneurship: You will work harder, make less money, and take longer to turn a profit than you ever imagined. Sorry, friends, I speak the truth. So if you are going into business to make lots of money, to work less, or get rich quick, you are going in for the wrong reasons.

Why did you go into marriage?

For some women, the answer really might be for economic security. The problem is that women have a ninety-seven percent chance of being the sole provider sometime during their lives (think divorce or death of a spouse), so that might not be the best reason to marry. To experience lifelong romantic bliss? Research is pretty clear that the fabulous rush of romantic love that comes at the beginning of a new relationship is not hormonally possible to maintain over a lifetime. We all will settle into a different, less charged kind of relationship over time that is a very different sort of love. Yet so many couples believe that biological high is what they are marrying for. How about to have children and a family? What happens if you can't have children or—God forbid—lose your family?

Schaefer highlights several more appropriate reasons for starting a business. I think they are great reasons for forming a marriage, as well.

a. You have a passion and love for what you'll be doing. You strongly believe—based on educated study and investigation—that your product or service would fulfill a real need in the marketplace. Remixed for marriage, that would read: You have a passion and love for the marital commitment and strongly believe—based on real conversation and discovery— that this relationship would truly fill a need for you and your love. That is a high bar, one a lot of folks don't ever consider on their way to the altar.

b. You are physically fit and possess the needed mental stamina to withstand potential challenges. We all took the vow, in sickness and in health, but this should be a real consideration in a long-term relationship. By this I mean that the marriage's health is truly affected by the physical and mental health of the partners so working to maintain mental and physical well-being should be regarded as key ingredients to success. When a partner is struggling with a health issue, it cascades into all aspect of the marriage—from time and financial resources to relationship challenges associated with caregiving and support. And if either of you is ignoring your health or doesn't consider it a priority, you really are risking your marriage, as well. Place a real priority on keeping your

physical and mental health. Come into a marriage with a clear understanding of the mental and physical health challenges that each of you might bring. Businesses fail when owners aren't able to give the time, attention and energy needed to sustain a healthy bottom line; same thing can happen in marriage.

c. You have drive, determination, patience, and a positive attitude. Enough said.

d. Failures don't defeat you. You learn from your mistakes. In marriage, I believe this is crucial. Over the years, Martin and I have made many mistakes. If we didn't have a real desire to succeed in our relationship, we probably would have failed at it. But maybe more important than wanting to keep going is learning from mistakes and making appropriate changes. Changing to meet the needs of the relationship in its present form is crucial to success.

Point No. 2: Another reason businesses fail is poor management.

Lacking expertise in the areas of financing, purchasing, process, or dealing with employees is a major downfall for many businesses. It is for marriage as well.

We know that financial issues are a main source of discontent in marriage. So many folks don't know how to budget, plan, or purchase when they reach adulthood. This is a major factor in marital problems. And when it comes to management, knowing how to manage children is a crucial factor in succeeding at marriage.

Under poor management, Schaefer also cites neglect. How often have you heard that a relationship fell apart because one partner simply lost touch with the needs of the other? Or both partners simply stopped thinking about and caring for the relationship. Businesses can fail when they are neglected by their principals; marriages certainly do.

Schaefer also mentions a poor work climate. Do you focus on creating the best possible home environment for your family? Virginia Satir, a pioneer in family therapy, wrote that designing a home environment where the family members want to spend time should be a major priority in every family's life.

Point No. 3: Insufficient capital is another factor in business failure.

If we learned one thing from the Great Recession of 2008, it's that families who got into houses they couldn't afford are at great risk emotionally and physically. The decision to have children has a huge economic impact on a couple. Did you consider that when you decided to begin your family? Is your family sufficiently capitalized?

The ancient Greeks understood that life might best be described as a hero's journey—a series of unfolding challenges and opportunities, in which the protagonist succeeds through skill, cunning, and bravery in the face of adversity. Schaefer's reasons for business failure reveal that we often lack the skill or strength—material, mental or physical—to overcome the obstacles that line our path.

The same is true of marriage. Success on this hero's journey requires indefatigable effort, skill, attention and, sometimes, bravery. Avoiding the common pitfalls can help to determine your success.

Plan Your Marriage's Ideal Future

You evaluate dangers, opportunities, and strengths for your business. Why not apply those principles to your marriage?

*I*n our brand-marketing business, we are keenly aware that in order to maintain relationships with our clients we must continually create value that helps them advance, grow, and meet their goals. To define "value," we've come to rely on the D.O.S. (Dangers, Opportunities and Strengths) conversation tool from Dan Sullivan's entrepreneurial development program, The Strategic Coach.

But can this practice be used in our personal lives as well?

At Thoma Thoma, we ask our client to visualize in detail an immensely satisfying future for himself or herself—casting the frame three years ahead. We then ask them to inventory the greatest dangers they face in reaching this future. From there, we investigate present opportunities and inventory the strengths they perceive now within their current organization. As we create a marketing communications plan for clients, we define strategies to systematically remedy dangers, capitalize on opportunities and leverage strengths.

I was reviewing a D.O.S. conversation with a client when I had a small epiphany—about my life partner, Martin. *I should be highly motivated to add value to his life and help him create his best future*, I thought. *Why don't I have a D.O.S. conversation with him?*

Making it Personal

So on our next business trip, I took advantage of a few spare hours I had alone in the car with Martin and conducted the D.O.S. interview. Martin described an ideal future in which there were no vestiges of the Great Recession in our business. We had the resources to travel, save, grow, and otherwise feel free of cash-flow stress. We had partners at Thoma Thoma who were sharing the load of ownership and creating space for Martin to write another book and for me to complete my first one. Martin described himself meeting the emotional and physical needs of our family. We'd be empty nesters and out from under most of the expenses related to college.

Dangers to achieving this picture included some powerful material. Supporting and caring for our parents might put this future at risk. (This served as a good reminder to formulate a plan with our siblings for this eventual reality.) Furthermore, as we experience an empty nest, we could grow apart rather than regain our identity as a couple—becoming "more partner, less spouse."

We also talked about the danger associated with either of us or one of our children becoming sick. This exploration might not sound like fun, but we found it motivating to seriously consider measures we could take that would lessen these risk factors.

Next, we identified many opportunities for ourselves as a couple. There would be fewer child-rearing expenses and less responsibility, as well as more freedom to explore personal interests such as traveling and writing. We love to mentor, and we foresaw opportunity to be a powerful influence in the lives of young people in our area schools and universities.

Naming our strengths—including health, relative wealth, and great friendships—was humbling and encouraging. Our ideal future was achievable. It was well within our ability to realize, even through the dangers that threaten to throw us off course. We realized we just needed a clear plan and path.

Charting the Course

That is the next step in the D.O.S. conversation. Sullivan suggests that while the conversation itself is valuable and insightful, the resulting plan and path are the vehicles that truly deliver value to the relationship.

I've seen the excitement in the eyes of our clients as they receive our suggestions for achieving their ideal futures and overcoming the obstacles to their business success. My goal was to provide such a plan and path to Martin and see how he reacted to my thoughts.

I have to admit this was an inspiring exercise. After so many years, it's easy to go on autopilot. What's working keeps working, and what isn't working gets pushed under the rug. The risk is that any danger trigger can send the ugly stuff shooting out from hiding and morph it into a monstrous, deal-breaking issue.

The structure of the conversation gave us a reason to stop long enough to evaluate our life situation. The plan and path gave us the impetus to act on the material that we know is important but doesn't feel urgent. And work on that material we did.

Looking back to the D.O.S. conversation I had with Martin, I am gratified by what we accomplished from the plan we made to address our D.O.S. findings.

Recognizing that we were likely facing a near future with parents who might need our support and care, we had substantive conversations with our mothers, both of whom are determined to live well, long, and independently. Martin's mother made some adjustments to her estate and will based on the conversation she and Martin had. My mother invested in a newer, safer car. We have a clear understanding of what they want and need from us in these later years, and that gives us a sense of focus and purpose.

I know that you are thinking that Martin and I really couldn't be much more tied at the hip as business partners, parents, and spouses. But the truth is, we—like all our friends with empty nests—had to redefine our relationship. We needed more than work and the kids to talk about at night. We needed a sense of coupleness that would make our post-childrearing life together more vibrant. Learning how to date again, as well as put a moratorium on business talk over those dates, helped tremendously.

What we really focused on was reevaluating our family budget with an eye toward the long-term ... money for one more kid to get through college, for travel, for retirement and debt repayment. Looking back this was a game-changer; we got more disciplined, did some deep, long-term planning with a financial advisor, and got to work on retirement plans.

Inspiring—all of this forward motion really *can* be traced back to that D.O.S. conversation we had while driving to a business meeting across the state. So many things in business and marriage result from deep conversation and taking the time to ask and answer hard questions.

Set aside a few hours, or catch your significant other in the car or on a plane and ask the D.O.S. questions. It's a powerful framing conversation in business. And as I've learned—in the Business of Marriage as well.

Judge But Don't Be Judgmental

Leave out the emotion. Look at your data objectively to determine the best course of action.

Anyone who owns or manages a business knows that making tough decisions lies at the core of the job. And in a milieu marked by instantaneous communication and the strain of recession, the decisions just keep getting more difficult.

Those same stressors affect our personal lives and relationships. How do we get the job done at home when we are busier than ever, unable (or unwilling) to disconnect from the constant stream of incoming communications, and faced with the reality or threat of fewer resources? It's a perfect storm. A tough decision can suddenly turn home into a battlefield where each partner is wounded by friendly fire.

Recent business decisions confronting Martin and me have required more attention, negotiation, and granularity than ever before. The stakes are high; we don't have a cushy net. Needless to say, it's made for interesting pillow talk.

We're forging ahead by using a principle we (or at least my husband) only recently identified: we must act with discernment, not judgment. Just what does that mean?

Here's my line of thought.

On the face of it, a judgment should be a fair and accurate weighing of the evidence to determine an outcome. In a court of law, evidence is presented and a judgment, or decision, is made. However, there is another kind of "judgment": the act of judging people, facts, situations, or experiences through the discoloring lens of emotion, opinion, or your own personal baggage. Think "judgmental." That little "–al" tacked onto a perfectly appropriate decision-making tool can mess up a decision—and a relationship—very quickly.

When emotion and personal opinion take over, we can become judgmental. We blame others and take problems personally. Not a good frame of mind for making high-quality, high-stakes decisions.

Call to mind an experience in which you and your partner held opposing opinions about a topic. Say you want to spend spring break on the sunny beaches of Cozumel. In your opinion the best, most delightful, most exciting and economical way to get there is by cruise liner. Your partner's opinion is that cruise liners are the most boring, claustrophobic, snail-paced way to get to the Mexican Riviera. Who is right? How will you decide? What is that conversation going to be like?

If you attempt to decide using these very emotional and personal opinions, you'll likely end up not just disagreeing but fighting. You'll either end up at home for spring break because you couldn't reach a decision, or the decision will be so charged that one of you will be burning up on the beach … and not from the subtropical sun.

Now let's talk about discernment. What I'm referring to here is the ability to look at objective information or inputs and determine the best course of action. This means slowing down to gather as much objective data as possible. You would determine in great detail what a successful outcome for the decision would look like, and then use the inputs to discern what course of action will come closest to creating the optimal outcome. In my experience, this approach simply requires—first and foremost—an agreement between the partners that you will approach the material with discernment and not judgment.

All right, now let's plan a vacation. Using discernment, we first agree that we want to go on vacation for one week over spring break. We agree that Mexico, specifically Cozumel or a similar beach, is the destination and that we would like to enjoy the journey as well as the destination. We look at our budget; how much are we willing and able to spend? What are our optimal arrival and departure times? How do we want to deal with food? Entertainment?

Armed with this level of information—and agreement—you might come to the conclusion that the cruise really is the best way to meet the majority of your desires for the money. Or perhaps the facts point away from a cruise toward a vacation

package at a trendy, all-inclusive resort. Either way, if you approach the options without being judgmental, it's more likely you'll be able to discern a decision that is agreeable to both of you. Martin and I have seen this work time and again. When we find ourselves caught up in making a hefty judgment, we back up, dig out some objective facts or data, return to our decision without holding so tightly to our precious opinions and— voilà—the decision is clear and acceptable to both of us.

In decision-making, details matter and facts matter. Discernment is an internal process. Good decision-making is a dance in which we can use our guiding principles to filter through the data to reach the best outcome. Self-management guru Stephen Covey called it "integrity in the moment of choice."

So the next time you and your partner find yourselves caught in an argument, you might try asking, "Are we making a proper judgment, or is there a bit of the judgmental involved in this?" Try backing up and starting from scratch with more information and less opinion. Reaching your decision through discernment may yield a way forward that makes you both happy—and happier with each other.

The Good to Great Marriage

How to be a hedgehog at home.

*G*ood to *Great,* Jim Collins' breakout business bestseller, is required reading for anyone in management, and it has been a go-to guide for me since its arrival in 2001. Collins' exhaustive research into companies that have succeeded markedly over time uncovered the attributes of true business leadership success. And it opened the eyes of many of us who generally believed that the best business leaders were the most aggressive, cunning, strategic—and maybe even a little ruthless.

Not so, according to Collins' research. Successful businesses are built by leaders who had more in common with a not-so-sexy woodland creature than its sleeker, more wiley woodland competitor. And this gives rise to the famous Hedgehog Concept.

Collins is paralleling an ancient poem in which the smart, scheming fox tries all sorts of ways to capture the hedgehog for his lunch. Meanwhile the hedgehog simply uses the same escape mechanism to win the lunchtime battle; he basically stops, drops and rolls—into a bristly ball. The poem puts it this way: "The fox knows many things, but the hedgehog knows only one thing." Of course, that one thing is the very thing that helps him win against the fox every time!

According to Collins then, having a hedgehog concept—or knowing the one thing that matters and sticking to it—is key to great companies' successes.

To quote: "Hedgehogs see what is essential, and ignore the rest."

So I've been thinking about how the Hedgehog Concept might apply to marriage. Could you, using a marital hedgehog concept, transform your marriage from merely good to stunningly great? It's certainly worth considering.

Here's the breakdown of the concept for business. The hedgehog principle lies at the nexus of three interlocking points of knowledge: knowing what you are deeply passionate about, understanding what you can be best in the world at, and knowing what drives your economic engine. We worked through these three questions at Thoma Thoma, and the result led to our becoming very focused on helping our clients to "live their brands." This has been a guiding principle in our company ever since, helping us to survive two major recessions and develop a unique expertise.

Let's explore how this concept might work in marriage.

First, we need to evaluate what we are passionate about as a married couple. Now thinking through this would make for a juicy conversation. What drives our marriage and our desire for marriage? For some, I think that driving passion might be to create a family. Some are passionate about marriage as an expression of their religious faith. For some it might revolve around generating self-knowledge through the shared relationship. Some folks value shared history or shared adventures as their passion. Others may be driven to have the stability that marriage brings.

Lots of us went into marriage passionate about passion, and sexual passion or life passion is a worthy desire.

Martin and I agree that the driving passion for us is to become what Gary Zukav calls true Soul Mates—or spiritual partners, aimed at reaching our highest personal potential through our marital relationship.

This is truly valuable knowledge to have about yourself, what drives you and energizes you to be married. It is a great thing to remember and hang on to during rough sailing—knowing the juice behind your decision to commit to marriage with each other.

What can you be best in the world at? This one is tricky in marriage, but again, what a terrific conversation to have with your mate—a discussion of what the two of you *together* are really, really great at! What can your pairing offer that others just can't? Now this is exciting!

Martin and I have a unique relationship that functions at its best when we recognize that we have the same interests and values, but complementary skills and approaches. Martin has mad skills that are weaker in me, and vice versa. We often create the most value when we work on projects together and we see this in our parenting success, in our business success, and in our success out in the community.

We are just better working together! Not all married couples can claim that to be true. And this is a good thing to remember as we decide what we want out of life.

The last point of knowledge seems tricky to decipher in a marriage. What drives your economic engine? I'm not used to thinking about my marriage in economic terms. Another way to ask it is, how do you add value to people's lives? How does this marriage add value to my life? My spouse's life? My children's lives? My community or my world?

When we thought about this one, we had to dig deep. I mean, really, what is the value being generated by the Thoma family being the Thoma family? At its essence, the value we derive from our marriage is that it has been the foundation or launchpad from which to soar. Our approach to parenting was to create this safe, firm foundation that would launch loving, happy, healthy, productive adults into the world for the greater good. Our marriage has launched our personal careers and has resourced our dreams for four decades. We've tried to be that safe foundation for our friends when they were in need to lean on us and take refuge or seek aid in order to move ahead with their lives.

Taken all together, through this marriage, Martin and I are compelled to reach our highest personal potential utilizing our unique ability to work together to create a launchpad for our success and that of others.

So every time I am challenged by life and am frantically looking for the "right thing to do," I should recall my marital Hedgehog Principle, turn toward my husband, take a deeper look at how this experience is challenging me on a deeper level, explore ways we can work together to meet this challenge, and look for how meeting it might create the foundation for something new and powerful in our lives. Rolling up into that prickly little ball doesn't sound weak, it sounds like real strength. Come on, foxes, I'm ready!

The Circle of Life
in Business and in Marriage

Learning to say Hakuna Matata to change.

*A*t this writing, Martin and I are four decades into our marriage and more than three decades into our business. I'm not sure which has changed faster. We began our business together as a creative team out of the back bedroom of our house—I was the designer and Martin the writer. Before long we were in rented space with two employees. We were beginning to consult and develop marketing plans for our clients, and we were running a small newspaper.

Then came steady growth into a creative boutique with a dozen or so staff, and we were not the writer/designer but the sales force and the management. Today we are the principals and managers of a unique brand leadership consultancy. I don't have design software on my computer, and Martin hasn't written copy for a creative project in years.

We survived the "dot-com bomb" and the greatest of modern recessions by adapting and changing at every turn.

Now we've begun the process of planning for our retirement and creating a succession plan. The only constant for decades has been constant change. And our marriage has been no different.

We began married life as college students working three jobs and managing full course loads. After college we moved to

Little Rock and began work. Starting a family threw us into the jaws of change and redefined every aspect of our lives and the roles we played at work and at home. Adjusting and adapting to the parenting of teenagers and young adults also meant grappling with our identities as a couple. Not too many years ago, I received a health diagnosis that rocked both Martin and me to the core. And now we are shifting to how to care for our aging parents—and preparing to learn to care for each other through health challenges and as we age. Nothing really stays the same.

If you study business or product life cycles, you note great similarity between the phases of a product or business and the phases of a marriage. Each phase poses challenges and opportunities and can be a great way to think about the challenges and opportunities in marriage. Borrowing from Thierry Janssen of the Just in Time Management Group, we can look at seven stages of business development and draw some useful parallels to married life.

The first stage is the "seed" stage, when the business is just an idea and partners are beginning to bring that business to life. The focus here is on determining if the business or product is a good fit, what resources can be brought to bear, timing, and creating a good business plan. Likewise, the "seed" stage of a committed relationship requires couples to determine if they are indeed a good match for one another. Are they compatible? Do they have passion around similar things or lifestyles? Are they both ready to be in a committed relationship at this time, and are they in a place where they can relocate if necessary? Now is the time when they need to open the books and share their financial situation and their money management style with their partners. Janssen notes that a critical success factor for businesses in this very new phase of development is a good business plan. We've talked about marital planning in this book, and I do believe there are crucial discussions that constitute a good "marital plan" for couples as they explore getting into bed together—no pun intended. These discussions include future vision and dreams, children or no, values, morals, and ethics around fidelity and sexual intimacy, spirituality and religion, and that all-important money and finance talk.

Now we've tied the knot and can consider ourselves a start-up marriage! In the "start-up" phase of the marriage we are doing what many new businesses are doing, creating the processes and protocols that will make the new venture run without a hitch. When partners are involved in a new business there is usually a period of adjustment and solidifying of roles. You'll find that period of adjustment in any marriage as well—experts call it negotiating the "power struggle." What are our roles in this relationship? Who has the power and under what circumstances? This is

MARRIAGE
Seeds

PHASE ONE

the time in a business's life when the partners rely on the support of good mentors or consultants. And newly married or committed couples should absolutely consider some good marital counseling if they find themselves struggling with their roles or in any of the areas I mentioned above in the seed stage. Good counsel now will lay the foundation for success long-term. No one should assume they know right off the bat how to be successfully married, or that their crazy love will be the critical success factor. Smart business owners have mentors; married couples need them as well.

If all goes well, in business we begin to experience "growth and expansion," and resource management becomes a big factor as we adjust to meet rising demand for our products or services. Growth in marriage comes to play when we expand our families. Having children is the big growth no-brainer, but subtler forms of expansion occur as we adjust to new family members and a larger sense of shared burden. Even bringing on pets creates growth issues for couples!

This is the "family" life that we all have in our heads when we think about marriage—raising kids, "buying up," great vacations, putting money in the bank. It's a vibrant time for marriage but also comes with its fair share of challenges.

So now, just like in business, we're trying to find and allocate the necessary fiscal resources to pay for children and growing households, and we're adjusting our time and individual contribution in order to get it all done. Now's the time to consider outsourcing some work in order to maintain the quality of your relationship. That may mean getting extra child care or household help so that you aren't just a working machine. This is an easy time to put the relationship on autopilot, focus on the kids, and just try to get it all done. Carving out time and focusing on the marriage is difficult and yet is the very key to long-term success. You are laying down the patterns that will enhance the next few phases, so make that relationship a high priority.

Ready for more change? Because here it comes—in the form of "maturity." In business terms competitive demands are just as fierce, yet sales are plateauing or even beginning to fall off. The company may begin to downsize to adjust for a smaller market share. That sounds an awful lot like what happens when children mature and leave the home. Couples have an empty nest but may have aging parents or health concerns to deal with. We're not ready to retire just yet, but we're looking at each other and asking ourselves, "Now what?" What do we really want? What do I want for myself? A lot of marriages dissolve at this phase, and businesses routinely slide downhill and fold. Is it time to exit or to consider a new venture? Both business partners and marriage partners often face this question in this phase. Experts note that business owners need good counsel at this phase of business, and once again, many marriages could really benefit from counseling at this point.

I remember waking up after our youngest son moved to college, looking at Martin, and thinking, *Boy, it's a good thing I like you!* We're in this phase now and are really rediscovering what we want and need from each other. There is a realization that time is not on our side so much anymore. We can't wait any longer to really go after the things we want in life. How do we plan for the next phase?

Enter the "exit" or "harvest stage" of business or products. Good planning can mean cashing out or selling the business and allowing the legacy to live on. What impact do we want to make on the future? How do we want to be remembered? Do we have the resources to handle what will happen over the years as we age? How will we face the end game together? This is heavy stuff, but as I watch my mother and mother-in-law navigate this phase, I can see them taking great pleasure in curating the family history, spending true quality time with their grand- and great-grandkids and enjoying each moment as it comes.

My recent diagnosis has put this phase of marriage a bit at risk, so I value this phase more than ever. I'm fighting for it, really. It won't be for the faint of heart, it will be about letting go. But it is a phase I don't want to miss—and I want to experience it with Martin—my partner in business and in life and in every phase of our relationship.

Communications

Healthy Conflicts Move You Forward

There's a difference between debate and fighting, and only the former is healthy.

Our Thoma Thoma leadership team meets off-site quarterly. Afterward, we digest and activate the decisions we make. These meetings are always productive—we quickly reach decisions that might drag out for weeks in the office. Strange as it may seem, I think what makes these sessions work is the passionate debate.

Debate. Well, maybe I should be more descriptive. We disagree. We argue. We speak up. We're heard. We move forward. Healthy conflict is one hallmark of an effective meeting. I also believe it has a vital role to play in marriage, and I'll argue with anyone who disagrees.

Here's why I believe in healthy conflict: for more than three decades, I've led meetings with all sorts of team dynamics in play. And I've noticed that really passionate, engaged people speak up and argue their points. Being heard is important to those who are truly engaged and invested in the outcome. I've also watched people who avoid the heat (and discomfort). It's not that hard; they simply disengage. They don't fight, but they don't engage. They are simply checked out—not married to the goals, you might say. Not committed.

I've also been party to horrible business conflicts where participants get so ugly, personal, and emotional they can't focus on the true discussion points. I've witnessed name-calling and people storming in and out of rooms, slamming doors, and raising voices. These encounters leave blood on the floor and relationship damage that lingers long after the details of the disagreements have been worked through. That's just plain old fighting. And it hardly ever works.

But disagreeing—arguing—works. It's the natural outcome of commitment and passion. Teams that aren't afraid of a healthy debate make decisions far more effectively and efficiently than those that avoid conflict, as Patrick Lencioni noted in his book, *The Five Dysfunctions of a Team: A Leadership Fable* (San Francisco: Jossey–Bass, 2002).

In his book, Lencioni names "fear of conflict" as a dysfunction because healthy conflict is required for relationships to grow. According to Lencioni, teams that fear conflict have boring interactions, create more back-channel politics and personal attacks, ignore the tough topics that are often critical to success, fail to tap into the perspectives of all team members, and waste time and energy. Healthy conflict, on the other hand, leads to lively meetings that extract all opinions, solve problems quickly, minimize the politics, and put critical topics on the table.

Because Martin and I spend so much of our lives working together with others in the room, we have developed a pretty good ability to argue effectively. In business, you just don't have the option of screaming and yelling. Developing a controlled, just-the-facts approach to arguing revealed to Martin and me that the more emotional tactics we might have deployed at home weren't very effective but certainly had the potential to hurt.

When we do lose it and fight nasty, one habit we've developed is to say, "We're on the same team here." This little code phrase helps us both remember that if one of us loses, we've probably both lost on some level.

All Parties Have to Be Heard

We've never been shy about a good, healthy debate over the dinner table or in front of our children, because we are by and large pretty good about sticking to the topic and reaching an agreement. Sometimes it's a compromise, but not always, because research has found that having your views truly heard and considered is as important as the final outcome. So sometimes, one of us loses. But always, both of us are heard.

This is imperative in a good relationship. The only thing accomplished by storming out and maintaining cold, stony silences is to prolong the issue and leave room for real damage. The tension and emotion from a good, healthy argument can be uncomfortable. But it need not cause any real, lasting damage to a relationship.

One tool that many businesses use is the Thomas–Kilmann Conflict Mode Instrument (TKI). This instrument helps people define their responses to conflict to determine how they behave most often: competing (assertive and uncooperative), accommodating (unassertive and cooperative), avoiding (unassertive and uncooperative), collaborating (assertive and cooperative), or compromising (moderately assertive and cooperative).

Understanding these ways of dealing with conflict can help you have a conversation about how you might work toward collaborating or compromising in an argument rather than competing, avoiding, or always accommodating (which can lead to underlying resentment).

Two questions to ask yourself if you find the discussion getting heated:

1. **Are the right people in the room?** In other words, is this appropriate at the dinner table in front of the kids? Am I dragging people into a disagreement they don't need to be a part of?

2. **Is this the right time for this?** Sometimes setting a time to discuss a disagreement can help both of you come together in the spirit of collaboration and compromise rather than aggression. This is also helpful if one of you is angry or unhappy but the other isn't aware of that. Confronting someone with a disagreement can be risky if he or she is not ready or able to listen or be listened to. Set aside time, and you'll be able to work out the problem more easily.

So don't shy away from conflict. It's the natural outgrowth of a passionate, involved relationship. Just remember that most people will compromise or work toward a solution that works for all if they truly feel heard and respected along the way. That's something we want at home as much—or more—than at work.

Why Business and Marriage Partnerships Fail

Everyone makes mistakes, but these
four could sink the partnership.

I have to smile inwardly whenever someone praises my business/marriage partnership with Martin as "so amazing." Has our history been a steady rise—a rosy bed of posies filled with passion, ardor, wealth, adventure, and bliss? Oh my goodness, no! I'd have to say our relationship track looks much more like an electrocardiogram. Lots of ups, just as many downs, and an awful lot of time in the "average" zone. Is that what "amazing" looks like?

An article by Amanda Neville in *Forbes* online magazine ("Why Partnership is Harder Than Marriage," March 2013) argues that business partnerships are harder than marriages. There's evidence to back this idea. While a whopping fifty percent of marriages will fail, an even more whopping eighty percent of business partnerships will ultimately end. Not great stats either way!

But I have to say that looking at my relationship with Martin through both lenses, I believe that marriage is the bigger, tougher commitment. I also see some striking similarities between the reasons these two types of partnerships fail—and the remedies that may help them succeed and stay the course.

Anne Field writes in *Business Insider* ("4 Fatal Mistakes Entrepreneurs Make When Taking on a Partner—And What You Should Do Instead") that four common mistakes are key reasons that business partnerships fail. As I consider these mistakes, I'd have to say that they also look like pretty consistent indicators of marital failure as well.

The first mistake, according to Field, is a failure to pinpoint roles. Often business partners fail to clearly define their roles within an organization. In a small business, it is common for the presidents or principal owners not to write a job description. They just do everything from sales to accounting to HR in an attempt to get the business going and keep it going. As the business grows and matures, this can create real conflict as partners break boundaries and step on one another's toes—whether in the area of sales or people management. Setting a clear definition of roles through detailed job descriptions or very clear role designation can keep partners on track and out of each others' lanes.

Similarly, I've seen and experienced the power struggle that comes with marriage as partners move from the romance phase into the day-to-day reality of living together and managing a house and family. Often individuals will simply adopt the roles their parents played in the primary household, doing those chores or managing the family money without a clear agreement around who will do what. I remember my shock at realizing that Martin really didn't actually reconcile his checkbook or truly keep any account of his cash flow. I quickly jumped in and "took control" of the money. After some deep (and often loud) conversations, our roles about money management morphed into a system that has worked well for us—much more a shared system than unilateral control, with each of us doing a very specific part. I'm the resource manager/purchasing agent, and he's the accountant. It works well for us, but it took some deliberate thought.

Things get truly complicated when kids enter the picture and the roles have to be redistributed again to make room for child rearing. Who will work? Who will stay home? How will we break down the care and feeding? It is no wonder that research reveals that couples are actually less happy with their marriages after the arrival of children. It's a recipe for role complication.

The second mistake business partners make is failing to discuss long-term goals. I've seen this blow up marriages as well. I remember a lovely couple who became dear friends. They were in Little Rock for the husband's medical school. As he was working toward residency, they were seriously contemplating medical missionary work. Both were very moved to give and to work for justice. But as the scenario of working in rural Africa became more real, my girlfriend, the wife, became more aware that this wasn't the life she really wanted—she was indeed frightened by the chaos and very real danger of African missionary work. Suddenly a marriage that had worked well during med school crumbled and dissolved as schooling came to a close. The two simply didn't agree on long-term goals.

It seems to me the biggest long-term goal that most couples need to discuss and get clarity on is whether they both want to have children—and how they plan to finance them. Another crucial decision focuses on *Where do we want to live?*—that is, *Am I going to be willing to move for your career?* Forks in the marital road don't spell success. Like it or not, you have to come to terms with a common, agreed-upon future.

The third mistake is a biggie: not stipulating how to make decisions or resolve disputes. I'd say that leads to marital break-up every bit as often as it leads to business partnership split. Determining how you will fight—and what is fair fighting—is just as crucial. While most of us would agree that abusive behavior— physical, verbal or mental—is off the table, many of us don't really discuss the finer points of arguing. Is yelling acceptable? Will we ever agree to disagree? Should conflicts always be resolved before bedtime? And exactly what is "fair fighting" anyway? Once again, our primary family patterns around conflict tend to become the model for our own conflict resolution and decision making. This can really backfire when families have different styles.

We have friends who scream and holler and then kiss and make up without remembering they had a problem the next day. We decided years ago that our marriage couldn't sustain that decibel level. We made an agreement to, in every way possible, keep the volume down. We haven't always succeeded, but it is part of our conscious rules for disagreeing. We also try to use the speech acts and courageous conversation guidelines detailed in the upcoming chapter on Low-Conflict Conflict Resolution.

A conversation around decision-making is a terrific idea. At Thoma Thoma, we use a system of management called The Entrepreneurial Operating System developed by Gino Wickman. We use Wickman's guidelines for decision-making within the firm. The management team offers various ways for resolving an issue, and then we put it to a vote. If there is a clear majority, then majority rules. If we are at an impasse, the person who is responsible for day-to-day business management (called the "Integrator" by Wickman) makes the decision. It's clear. It works. And no one gets upset. At home it's a little less black and white. If one or the other of us is the clear authority regarding the decision (me for decorating decisions, Martin for technology choices) then that person tends to make the final decision. For everything else, we turn to good old Stephen Covey and go for "Win-Win or No Deal." At least we know the rules we're playing by!

The final mistake business partners make is giving short shrift to the partnership agreement. It's surprising how many partnerships are not formalized in writing. The new business has all the proper terms and agreements, but the actual partnership terms are not solidified.

In marriage, I'd say this mistake goes one step further: the marital agreement (the vows) just isn't respected. Disaster.

Martin and I didn't draw up a pre-nup (although many of our happily married friends swear by theirs). But we have always deeply respected those altar vows and have had real clarity about the deal-breakers. Vows are easy to keep when everything is easy. But when sickness really does befall a spouse, or financial disaster threatens, or children are struggling, we really reveal our commitment to the agreement. Martin and I have been willing to struggle and fight and change to stay together. If either of us had lost that commitment, I wouldn't be writing this book.

Deal-breakers are real. Martin and I have a really short list, mostly around fidelity, personal treatment, and treatment of the kids. But we know what the line is and exactly how it's crossed. I guess you could say we understand our marital agreement and we've fought to stay true to it.

So which partnership is harder to maintain? Marriage or business? I'm still leaning toward marital as the trickier one, but I'm even more committed to avoiding the mistakes and nurturing the skills than ever!

How To Brand Your Personal Partnership

Apply a standard business principle to make a lasting marriage.

*B*randing. That ubiquitous marketing buzzword. Every business wants a brand; many businesses invest heavily in developing, promoting, and growing their brands. Martin and I have created a business devoted to building strong, magnetic brands. So it got me thinking: is there anything in the discipline of branding that might benefit a relationship?

The more I explored the question, the more interesting it became. Many folks have told me that Martin and I are a unique couple. They point to our ability to work together successfully. They marvel that for years we shared an office, working across a partners' desk.

There are, after all, some rather famous couple brands. How about Brangelina? Those political Clintons? The ever-expanding Duggars?

In our brand strategy work, we help our clients identify and validate attributes that engender unique, sustainable, competitive advantages. It's hard work, but it yields the foundation for their brands.

The first filter is to determine and highlight what is unique about the product or service. For Martin and me, it is clearly our desire and ability to partner on so many levels. What is unique about your relationship? This is a fun question to ask, perhaps over a glass of wine. When I think about this question, I also think about how Martin and I were very young when we married. I was twenty; I could get married but not drink in a bar.

I also think about our courtship. We dated six weeks before we were engaged; ten days later, Martin flew to Southeast Asia, where he spent the next six months. Not every couple has a court-ship story like this!

Having identified those unique facets of your relationship, now ask yourself, "What is sustainable about our relationship?" This is a tougher question. When I look at how young we were when we married, I can hardly say this attribute is terribly sus-tainable. I recently learned that while half of marriages end in divorce, the success rate for couples wedding in their teens or early twenties dips even lower—to about a thirty-five percent success rate.

Certainly the fact that we had a short courtship is not the sus-taining thread that has brought us through to the present day.

But that impulse to partner, to work together closely in most areas of life—that, I would say, is definitely a key to our ability to sustain our marriage.

So now I'm left with one attribute that might "brand" my marriage. Will it pass the last test? Is it a competitive advantage? When we talk about products and services, we're really talking about how desirable the brand is to the marketplace. Does the market really value this, and will people purchase based on this attribute? So for the sake of our relationship discussion, I'll put it this way: is this something that other couples might value or desire to have in their own relationships?

Based on qualitative research (all the comments I've received over the years I've been in business and marriage with Martin), I'd have to say that this ability and desire to deeply partner is an advantage. Over the many challenges and changes that life can bring, many couples find themselves drifting apart toward disparate goals and aspirations.

Martin and I have, for better or for worse, been forced to stay in very close, focused alignment about our future. I remember a financial advisor telling us that we had a better chance of succeeding in a business partnership than most because the key to a successful business partnership is to hold the same future vision for the company. Since our future is always intrinsically linked, our chances of holding that marriage together are also greater, I believe.

So the Martin and Melissa brand might be summed up as a marriage in which we partner to bring about the best possible life for ourselves and our family; and we couldn't do it as well without each other.

We even have a tagline. When we were engaged (those first ten days before Martin flew away), we assured each other that we were going to have "A Sky Blue Life." It was a literary reference to what we recall was a Guy de Maupassant story, though we cannot find it now. A Sky Blue Life is full of promise, has no limits, and is mostly sunny. Sure, it's the vision of a couple of starry-eyed twenty-year-olds. But I still love the ideal, and it suits us perfectly, even today.

So what's your relationship brand? Try your own brand-definition project using our unique, sustainable, competitive advantage filter.

Uncovering the brand within is always affirming and energizing for a business leadership team. The same can be true for you and your partner. What a beautiful gift to give to one another. Explore the foundations of your personal relationship brand and see how that understanding adds real energy to your partnership.

Marriage by Memo

You put everything on paper and
assign action items at work. Why don't
you do that with your family at home?

*I*n business, I've come to believe that ninety percent of success
boils down to clear communication. The quality of communication between customer and company predicts the quality of client
service. We rely on accurate communications to make agreements, give instructions, strike deals, and negotiate compensation. The wheels of any organization can fall off if communication
gets bungled, boggled, or blown.

Most verbal exchanges made in the business environment are
reiterated or enhanced by written communications. I give verbal
instructions to my teammates regarding client feedback and then
follow up with an e-mail. After our weekly client meetings, we
follow up immediately with action items detailing agreements,
accountabilities, and deadlines. We shake hands over a contract
we've initialed. We take notes during a meeting and then distribute those to the group afterward. We do all of this because we
understand that clear communication makes the wheels go
'round. Without it, we're out of a job.

So just how important is clear communication in a marriage? A
column by Thom W. Conroy says it well: "In any relationship, the
cornerstone of understanding another human being lies in the

ability to communicate and, lacking this, a relationship is superficial at best" ("The Importance of Communication in Relationships," Relating360, March 7, 2009). Since marriage is no "superficial relationship," I'm on solid ground claiming that clear communication is an absolute imperative.

So why don't we take another page from the playbook of business and bring more written backup into our marriages? Wouldn't that take us far in increasing clarity and understanding?

When you sit down to talk about something important with your partner, how often do you take notes? In business, most of us take notes habitually while engaged in any conversation. I walk around Thoma Thoma with a small orange notebook (because orange makes me happy) and scribble notes about every conversation I have. And it's a pretty good thing, because more often than not, I find myself returning to those notes to clarify a detail or date that slipped my mind—or to see if I promised to do something I have since forgotten. The practice is a lifesaver. I think my larger-than-wanted posterior is due to the extremely effective way my note-taking covers my backside.

But at home, I rarely take notes. I rely on my perimenopausal brain to remember everything (which is dangerous). Without that pen-to-paper effort, I may not be listening quite as carefully to what Martin is saying.

Have you ever entered into a contract with your child? Funny—we negotiate with our kids all day, every day, to greater or lesser effect. But if you have ever drafted a written agreement about, say, use of the car or the weekend curfew, you have probably noticed that those agreements seem to stick more often. It's hard for a preadolescent to argue that he or she didn't understand that midnight did not mean "any time convenient between midnight and one a.m." when you have talked through a written document and then both signed it.

At Thoma Thoma, action items are the lifeblood of the agency. A wise consultant once taught us that breakdowns at work usually happen when "you don't fulfill a request I didn't make." He reiterates that true agreements require a clear request, a clear consent to the request, consensus on criteria for completion, and a deadline. Action items are the written response to agreements made during meetings and interactions. They involve the action, the person responsible, and the deadline. These are effective, hard-working documents that ease stress, grease the wheels, reduce conflict, and clarify conversations.

So why haven't I ever used action items at home? I'm thinking about this because recently I raced out of town with so little prep time that I missed any kind of conversation with Martin or my son, Sam, about what needed to happen in my absence—and who needed to do what to cover all the bases. So I wrote a long, detailed memo to Martin and Sam and e-mailed it. Just for good measure, I printed it and posted it where they would be sure to see it … right on their dinner plates.

Guess what? I got home to find the printed memo all marked up. It had aided their suppertime discussion and planning for the following days without Mom. It was marked up with notes about who would do what. Items were systematically checked off. Everyone was fed, clothed, washed, entertained, and caught up on school and work. It was wonderful. No harried, nagging conversation between two adults who are on their way out the door for the day and really are only able to track about half of the information being downloaded. Just a memo. Sweet.

So that's it! I'm going to start using action items to keep my family in the know about who expects what and when. That's just good communication.

Etiquette for Home and Office

These ten rules instill civility everywhere.

Wouldn't it be great if our partner were perfect? If he or she behaved according to plan and met our needs while eliminating annoying habits and getting more charming every year? I'm pinching myself now—back to reality after staring dreamily out of my office window.

Let's be honest: some of the behavior we exhibit at home would get us fired or sued at work. We understand that in business it's necessary to measure our words and guard our actions—otherwise the wheels fall off. Why aren't we willing to demonstrate similar restraint in our personal relationships? After all, business etiquette reflects our understanding that aggression, meanness, teasing, name-calling, and sexual objectification are not okay.

Working as business partners has taught Martin and me important lessons about how we temper behaviors at both home and work. While our intimate relationship enables us to be honest and direct at work, the few times we've stepped over the line and gotten angry with each other, we quickly saw how upsetting and damaging it was to our co-workers. We just don't have the luxury of creating an emotional mess to clean up. Folks can't work effectively or efficiently under that stress.

That office experience made me notice that the same thing was happening at home with our children when we lost our tempers. They were scared, stressed, and confused. Do we disagree in front of the kids? You bet. But we follow the same rules we follow at work. We stay calm. We don't shout. We listen carefully, and each allows the other to be heard. Then we start to negotiate. If it is a volatile situation, we take it offline, away from others.

I'm no Moses, but being the polite Southern girl that I am, I offer the following Golden Rules for Universally Good Behavior— at home or work.

Rule 1: Do what you say you will do.

Most of us know that if we agree to a request at work or make an agreement with a client, we have to follow through. Why is it so easy to make a promise to your partner and then let it slide (be honest)? We've all felt the injustice, the erosion of trust and the frustration engendered when we break this rule. We need to treat our partners with equal respect.

Rule 2: Be on time.

Sounds simple. Why don't more people follow this one? In the working world, those who are repeatedly late earn the scorn, mistrust, and disrespect of their co-workers, clients, and vendors. Being on time confers respect. It says quite clearly, "You are important to me." Is your partner's time as important to you as your own time?

Rule 3: No name-calling.

Would you call your co-worker a stupid fool? Would you even say his idea was stupid? Don't go there with your partner. What's damaging at work is devastating at home.

Rule 4: No yelling, please.

You know you aren't supposed to yell at work. You aren't supposed to yell at home, either. If you lose your temper and yell at co-workers, you'll likely be spending some time in anger-

management class ... or on the street. It's not effective at work because it's not effective. Period.

A corollary: This extends to the kids, too. We don't yell at our subordinates at the office; we don't yell at our children, either.

Rule 5: Say "please" and "thank you."

This little courtesy makes for a pleasant atmosphere. Please begin a request with "please." Please acknowledge others' efforts with a "thank-you." Thank you.

Rule 6: Absolutely no electronic fights, diatribes, or one-way reprimands.

Have you noticed how easy it is to shoot off a nasty e-mail, text, or phone message? Don't go there. Ever. Please. We have a policy at our office that no content that is confrontational, negative, or emotionally laden will be shared by e-mail. These are face-to-face conversations. And no one is to use all caps to express themselves via e-mail. Digital communication is easily mistranslated, one-way, limited-context. Save electronic communication for facts, scheduling, keeping up. Not disagreeing.

Rule 7: If it's important, set an appointment.

Really. If Martin wants to have a deep conversation with me at six p.m. on Friday and all I can think about is a big glass of cabernet and five hours of *Friends* reruns, I just tell him we need to set an appointment. And we do. We typically come to these meetings (often on Sunday afternoon) with a much better attitude and an ability to really focus on that one important thing.

Rule 8: Respect a closed door.

When we encounter closed doors at work, we know that a meeting, important phone call, or just concentrated effort is happening on the other side. Do we barge in? Do we yell through it? No. We just knock. Teaching our children (and partner) to tap on a closed door at home can save so much embarrassment. It's a sign that I respect your right to a little space. So rather than barge in on you enjoying an afternoon bubble bath, I'll ask permission to enter your space. Nice.

Rule 9: Embrace "I'm sorry."

Funny, sometimes it's actually easier to apologize to folks we're closest to and beg off with every excuse at work. But acknowledging a mistake and apologizing for the results it caused are necessary to the long-term health of any relationship. Saying "I'm sorry" when we have caused someone to feel bad, whether we meant to or not, is the civil thing to do. It runs up all kinds of brownie points and deposits in the emotional bank account. "I'm sorry" acknowledges the damage, even when there was no ill intent.

Our policy at work is that when we make a mistake, we openly share it with the client, explain what went wrong and what we did about it, and how we will adjust our processes to avoid that mistake in the future. Try this at home.

Rule 10: The Golden Rule is always the best rule.

Enough said. It works at work, and it works at home.

Low-Conflict Conflict Resolution

Conduct "Courageous Conversations"
and resolve conflicts more agreeably.

Conflict is part of every human relationship. Make that every kind of relationship: I just glanced up from the monitor in time to witness our black cat swipe a sharp claw and hiss angrily at our rotund and lazy gray cat, who was hogging the windowsill. And while Bad Omen (another story) bullied his way to success with Murry, the same technique is not as effective with your partner.

Martin and I will are closing in on four decades of marriage. In that time we have engaged in more forms of conflict than I care to count—yelling, one-sided rants, lectures, bawling, note-writing, the silent treatment, and late-night come-to-Jesus talks. All of these have involved varying degrees of failure. But as is often the case, our business showed us a better way to discuss our problems. And we've used this technique at home with similar success.

A few years ago, we hired professional leadership coach Barry Goldberg to help us develop our management team. For one year we worked individually and as a group to learn the best ways to manage as a team. Goldberg introduced a script that we lovingly named "The Courageous Conversation." We now train the entire staff in this process, and it is the foundation for how we deal with conflict at Thoma Thoma.

Here is the process: the first imperative is to ask for a mutually agreeable time to have the conversation. Let your partner know that it is of the courageous sort and the nature of the issue. For example, "Martin, I need to have a courageous conversation around the issue of forgetting to pick up our child twice in one week. When can we talk about this?"

Proper scheduling is critical to success. Sometimes your partner will be ready to talk about it right then. Fine; do it. Other times he or she will prefer to regroup later. Fine; set the time. The idea is not to create a torturous period of anticipation. It is to create a "safe space" for the conversation to happen in a non-threatening manner. If the topic is a real button-pusher for your partner, it may be enough to say, "I need to have a courageous conversation," then introduce the topic at the actual time of the conversation. Once you have a mutually agreeable time, let it go. No goading, jokes, or under-the-breath muttering. Just wait for the conversation. Once you are sitting down for this discussion, begin like this: "Martin, Sam was left at school for an hour two times last week." (Just state the facts, please).

Take a breath and share this statement, filling in the blanks: "When you [do the behavior in question], I feel [how it makes you feel] and it makes me want to [behavior you want to respond with]. What I would prefer is [insert desired behavior here]."

Continuing my example: "Martin, when you forget to pick up Sam, I feel like I can't trust you and you don't respect me, and it makes me want to [scream, cry, take your head off, accuse you of being uncaring and immature]. What I would prefer is that you set an alarm on your phone or your computer so you don't forget Sam again."

Your judgment or opinion of a bad situation will likely be very one-sided and colored by your life experiences and past hurts. Your opinion may not have value or relevance to your partner based on his or her life experience and past hurts. So framing the conversation to describe how the behavior makes you feel is less arguable. It acknowledges your reaction without implying that the problem is anyone's "fault."

How you feel when someone does or says something is a fact, not a judgment. A grievance defined in this way encourages others to acknowledge your feelings (which most of us need, anyway) and encourages the two of you to simply address the problem.

In the above scenario, Martin might say, "I'm sorry about that; it makes me feel really bad, too. I'm just so stressed out about that deadline next week that I got wrapped up in my work and forgot the time. I'll try setting my phone alarm from now on."

He might also say, "I'm sorry you feel that way, but I don't think of this as a problem. Sam was not worried or upset. And I eventually remembered him." You then have a chance to listen and decide if you want to make an adjustment. You might just say, "This makes me too nervous and irritated; do you think you could set your phone alarm from now on?"

Here's what's notable about a conversation like this. The problem is framed without judgment or condemnation. I didn't say, "Martin, you absent-minded professor, you completely abdicated your responsibility as a parent twice last week by forgetting your son at school!"

The blame-free framing sets the stage for you to discuss a problem in which there isn't really any fault, only upset. For instance, I had to have a courageous conversation with Martin about his snoring, which was leaving me exhausted and angry. If I remember correctly, I said something like: "Martin, your snoring has become so severe that when you get going in the middle of the night, I feel out of control, and it makes me want to smack you over the head and sleep in separate beds." He got to the sleep clinic real fast and doesn't snore anymore.

If you stay on your courageous conversation script, you won't be tempted to bring up past grievances or issues. You won't get going on the "you've done this a thousand times" or the "you always do this" script.

If you are on the receiving end of a courageous conversation, you have several factors working for you. First, your partner didn't just walk up and start yelling. You have had a heads-up that there is a problem—and, in a general sense, the nature of that problem. You can be prepared. Your responsibility is to listen and offer your feedback about that issue along with encouragement to get past the problem to the solution.

Try this with a problem that arises at home. All you have to remember is your script: "When you [do the behavior in question], I feel [how it makes you feel] and it makes me want to [behavior you want to respond with]. What I would prefer is [insert desired behavior here]."

This conversation is indeed courageous—and also effective.

Master the Art of Partner Negotiation

Strengthen your relationship by negotiating
a win–win deal every single time.

We approach our work relationships with the natural understanding that we'll be assigning or receiving tasks, setting goals, giving or getting rewards, and determining our future in business through the process of negotiation. But we often fail to realize the extent to which we need this skill at home with our partners or children.

I attended a workshop on effective business negotiations, offered by one of my clients. The seminar featured Deepak Molhotra, associate professor at the Harvard School of Business. Martin and I participated in a role-play activity simulating a buy–sell negotiation for a piece of land to be developed. Our negotiation was quick, simple, and straightforward. More than one hundred pairs of negotiators squared off in that class. When the speaker revealed the dollar range of all the different agreements, I laughed. At either end of the spectrum, the buyer or seller could have exclaimed, "I was robbed." But neither Martin nor I had out-negotiated the other. There were no losers in the deal, only winners.

That may not be the best way to negotiate in business. Depending on the situation, you may decide to negotiate to a clear advantage. An article on the Mind Tools website (a source for career development and management training, mindtools.com) makes a good point: "Where you do not expect to deal with people

ever again and you do not need their goodwill, then it may be appropriate to play hardball." But as Molhotra pointed out, the process of negotiation is every bit as important as the outcome, because it's how you feel at the end that will determine whether you have a future opportunity with that partner.

When it comes to negotiating with your life partner, I'd wager that you'll be dealing with each other again, so why not determine that every negotiation should produce only winners and strengthen the relationship? Sadly, a lot of folks just want to play hardball at home. It's rooted in the classic power struggle that comes from learning to share a life together. Couples get so caught up in claiming their space on the lifeboat that they are willing to win at each other's expense. The only problem is, that parting shot is likely to put a hole in the lifeboat they're sharing.

Consider the principle of "win-win or no deal," articulated by Stephen Covey in *The 7 Habits of Highly Effective People*. According to Covey, the first thing negotiators should do is seek to understand. For example, if your partner is likely to approach the coming duck season with, "I'm going hunting next weekend," try to get beyond the facts to his real desires. Does he want that exact weekend or every weekend? Or does he want to guarantee that he'll have the chance to spend some quality time with his buddies in the duck blind?

Now you can negotiate to a mutually agreeable outcome. "I want you to have some time at the club as well, but next weekend is that dance recital for Mary and I feel that you should be there in support of our daughter. Let's look at the calendar and find the weekends that are good for everyone."

It is from the basis of understanding that you can move through the components of a successful win-win agreement:

- **Desired results:** not the method, but the desired outcomes and goals, the "I want to do this because …"

- **Guidelines:** the parameters we are willing to operate within. You might be willing to give him as many as three weekends away during duck hunting season, but not every weekend.

- **Resources to help accomplish the goal.** You might negotiate to invest in extra child care during the weekends he is hunting.

- **Accountability:** What are our standards? You promise not to cop an attitude as the weekend of hunting approaches. He promises to make sure his obligations to the family are met before leaving town each Friday.

- **Consequences:** He recognizes that you are due some girls' weekends after hunting season. You recognize that this may be tough, but you made a fair negotiation.

Be honest: Have you worked out a plan with your partner that reached this level of communication? So often, we don't get into the detail necessary to feel good about the solutions we come to in our personal relationships. What's needed is just this level of clarity.

Over the course of our business relationship, Martin and I have had to negotiate many things, from the correct marketing strategy for a client to our annual budget allocations. We've found that we do best when we:

- Are extremely clear (as in, "I do not agree with your proposed plan. We need to negotiate").

- Set aside a specific time to negotiate.

- Are clear about our parameters. We will absolutely not settle the deal without a true negotiated outcome.

Covey calls this approach "win-win or no deal." Neither of us moves forward with any plan until we have agreed on that plan.

Is there tension? You bet! Are we passionate about our positions? Yeah! But we're in the same boat, remember? It does one of us no good to win at the other's expense. So negotiate to a win-win, remembering that the alternative is no deal. You'll walk away the winner—and so will your partner.

The Family Social Media Policy

*In this brave new online world, every family
needs to set healthy boundaries.*

Privacy—what a concept! In this brave new social world we live in, how do we really expect to have and keep privacy and intimacy in any true sense of the word? Everyone struggles to set boundaries around their online persona, but it can be very hard to control this when anyone with a smartphone can snap a pic and tag you in a matter of seconds. I've cringed repeatedly when I opened my Facebook to find myself tagged in a less-than-flattering photograph taken at a gathering the night before. No one asked me if I wished to be tagged—my permission was assumed because, I guess, I agreed to be photographed.

Every half-thought-out comment or silly aside lives forever in that great mystery warehouse called "the cloud"—there for any HR person to "Google," or snoopy neighbor to "creep."

Businesses have had to confront a whole new world in which their employees' private lives are no longer private. As a result, they have wrangled with the edges of what they can and cannot ask employees to do on social media. Companies have worked hard to craft social media policies that create safe, legal boundaries for their employees. Walmart, for example, has a social media policy that meets the National Labor Relations Board's standards; it is worth taking a look at.

We've all heard horror stories about employees who have Instagrammed photos or created videos of themselves—in company uniform—using company products in, shall we say, creative ways. This can create a true brand crisis for the company, resulting in sales losses and legal battles. Domino's Pizza reported losses of a percent or two for the quarter after one such video went viral.

So crafting a social media policy for your family is really a requirement today. And I think it could be an eye-opening conversation for some.

I have a friend who recently married and was surprised by her new spouse's boundaries regarding privacy. He was very sensitive to sharing their whereabouts and social engagements. He didn't want everyone knowing every detail about how they had spent their weekend. He didn't want to give casual acquaintances or co-workers fodder for superficial conversation with him. It wasn't about what might be in the posts. It was about saving some of his life for himself. They've come to an agreement about what goes on social media that works well for them.

I've come to determine that for me, there will be no negative email, very little private posting, and only in-person conversations for any sensitive matters. My personal fallback plan is to try to say and do online anything I would be willing to say, do, or justify in public. I guess I lead my private life as though it were all public and hope that this will protect me.

A quick look at my own Facebook timeline reveals how differently each of my friends interprets an appropriate post to be. One friend maintains no Facebook presence whatsoever and tries to make known that she would rather not be identified in photos or comments posted online. One posts multiple times daily, keeping us all apprised of her travels, entertainment, dates, and musings in real time.

I have friends who share numerous photos and video of their little darlings. Some of them use their kiddos' proper names. Others give their children handles in an attempt to create a privacy barrier.

Many of my friends post political and religious opinions. I wonder if they assume we all share the same values and beliefs— or if they just don't care who they might offend. The issues are not just related to privacy; social media has security implications as well. Most of the time it is easy to tell who is away on a trip, a trick I've read is used by house-thieves to hunt down empty houses.

What are you comfortable having your spouse share about you or your relationship online? I have some friends who carry on a public "love" letter in their social pages. Are you comfortable with that? Do you want your political or religious views shared? Some couples are in ministry, and sharing their faith is natural. Not so much for others who are more private about their spiritual lives.

This conversation can extend to photos, videos, and email as well. At a community fundraiser, I honored a beloved TV and radio host in our town. This guy has given his time to help so many organizations raise money for charity as their auctioneer that by his count he has helped raise more than $31 million. His style is over-the-top, comedic roasting! I created a crazy rework of Beyonce's famous "All The Single Ladies" music video. And yes, I wore a skin-tight dance outfit, a long wig, and high heels to boot! There was a little posting—I was prepared for that. But if I woke up tomorrow to Martin reposting my "Beyonce" pictures and commenting with a flirty little something about "putting a ring on it," I would not be too happy.

When you have children, the social media policy needs to be put in place early and reviewed often. I researched family social media policies and found comments from parents whose kids had Twitter accounts at age four. So I mean "early" literally. There is a nice resource for creating a family policy from Alexandra Samuel of Love Your Life Online: http://www.alexandrasamuel.com/parenting/creating-a-family-social-media-policy. She reminds us that this isn't a legal document—most families don't need to sue one another over posts! But it is fairly comprehensive and will assure a great conversation.

Martin and I are both active on social media for business purposes but keep our personal lives pretty quiet online. Our children are adults now, but when they were teens, we were transparent about our right to read any posts, tweets, or texts. We paid for the phones, so we could check the content. For the most part, our kids' online lives were pretty tame. We did talk a lot about questionable photos at parties and stuff that might live on to haunt them. But if we were parenting today, we'd have a policy such as the one mentioned above.

Take time to talk about the details I mentioned earlier around photo sharing and email. I think it is always a good idea to ask the subjects of any photos if they are okay with being tagged and shared on social media.

Furthermore, commenting needs to be discussed deeply. We all need to be reminded that without the visual context of face-to-face or even voice communication, it is so easy to misread the intent of written words. Capital letters equate to shouting in print. Sarcasm and even gentle teasing can really go wrong here. As I said, my personal policy is to undertake no corrective or negative communication via email. For me, it's face-to-face or by phone if that's the only option. Our evolving brains are way behind our technology today; we need to connect in real time with real conversation.

Anthonia Akitunde, in an article for American Express Open Forum, outlined the elements of a good social media policy for businesses. Many elements are worth noting here for families as well.

First, the policy creates a safe space for employees to share their concerns. What a great way to encourage family members to connect and discuss issues that are bothering them in private, rather than going public with a rant about, say, Mom's stupid rules.

The policy also outlines what is considered confidential information. Again, ideas vary between family members about this, so talk it out and agree to the boundaries. It is clear about the consequences when the policy isn't followed. It discusses the proper way to communicate online, discusses what's legal, and educates. What a great conversation for families to have!

Social media is a gift. It has the potential to extend our voices and our reach globally. That is real power—and real freedom of expression. Are we mature and secure enough to understand and handle that power? And are we prepared to respect our spouse and our family in that brave new public world? Open the conversation and make some determinations so that you and your spouse can balance the privacy you desire with the social community you want.

Finance

Bring The Budget Process Home

The concepts that keep business cash flow in order can do the same at home.

It's the most argued about, most costly, most dangerous issue in most relationships. Money. Money is handled in a fairly straightforward way in the business world. We budget for it. We account for it. We invest it and spend it, and we have methods for safeguarding it. And we all know that the aim of a healthy business is profit. So let me ask you a question: how do you intend to profit from your relationship with your spouse or life partner?

Start by considering the "profits" you hope to reap as a couple or as a family. Through my marriage I hope to gain access to experiences that I might not have by myself. I profit from the ability to co-create on every level: from having children to building a business to creating a home environment and a lifestyle that are rich and satisfying. And it goes deeper than that. I will profit from having the support of my spouse in sickness and old age. This is no small list of profitable outcomes.

We expect such amazingly rich outcomes from our relationships. But do we budget, plan, invest, and safeguard our resources to ensure that we will be able to achieve them? Do we bring a businesslike discipline and mindset to producing results in our relationship? It makes sense to do so. Money is, after all, the number one area of conflict and cause of divorce in marriage.

Let's assume you've laid out a budget at home. Now let's talk about how to manage those budgeted finances. I'd suggest designating a CFO for the family. This is the person who is accountable for overseeing the family resources, the budget, investments, savings, and real assets (including cars and real estate).

Note that this person doesn't get to decide how it all gets spent; he or she primarily oversees and manages the finances. Martin is our family CFO. He tracks the financial and tax data that come into the household and makes sure the bills are paid on time. Why is he the CFO? Because he has the time and the attention to detail to be good at it. Does he decide how much money should be spent at this week's grocery run? No. We agreed on a budget together in December.

In a well-run business, the CFO doesn't approve the expenditure of every little penny. That is micromanagement, and it doesn't empower employees to use their insight or enable ideas to shine. At home it should be no different. Each of you should have discretionary budget amounts that you may spend freely without the input of the other. Likewise, you should agree to a cap on the dollars each can spend without the knowledge and input of the other. It's a purely personal decision. There's no right or wrong to it. That expenditure should be tied to that overall budget—no spending beyond your resources without a talk. But otherwise, we're free to take advantage of sales or deals, or to treat ourselves or the other to a gift.

I know that many couples have joint accounts and separate accounts with discretionary spending privileges. That's great. Still, couples should agree to an amount that they feel calls for a discussion even when it comes from those individual accounts. Consider a business. No matter who you are and what authority you have, there comes a level of investment or expenditure on which you'll seek counsel and agreement from other managers or owners. It's no different in the business of marriage. You might purchase a lovely new living room suite from your discretionary checking account, only to find that your spouse is infuriated because you have put the family at risk should one of you lose your job and you need to reassign your resources. Open financial books and open communication are the best ways to deal with money in marriage.

At Thoma Thoma, we practice "open-book management." Our employees all contribute to the bottom line. As such, they all have a right to know about our basic financial situation and how it impacts them. Even if you're keeping separate accounts, we recommend that anyone who is contributing toward a shared purpose (and contributing doesn't just mean dollars) has the right and the obligation to see the overall financial picture. Keep the books open, and be accountable to one another.

Smart businesses employ multiple financial professionals, from accountants to financial planners, to assist them with financial management. So should you. I really don't understand why

we don't have required classes in personal finance at the high school level to prepare us to run a household. Managing money is complicated, and most of us didn't learn much more than how to balance a checkbook (obsolete information these days, when we run our checking accounts off a debit card and internet banking). So seek as much counsel as you can from a trusted professional advisor. The two of you probably came to your relationship with different views about money and how to use it. Proper counsel can open you both up to new ideas about money and help you negotiate an agreement about how the two of you will use money together.

How can you assess the well-being of a company? Just look at the bottom line. The same can be said of a marriage. Any couple with financial trouble is undergoing stress that is potentially detrimental to the relationship. So don't wait another minute. Make this the year that you address your budget so you can start generating real profit in your marriage.

Marriage Pays

Being married is good for the bottom line. We explore possible reasons behind this finding.

According to the Census Bureau, lasting marriages create more wealth for their partners than single life. A fifteen-year study of 9,000 people found that those who married and stayed married during that time built up nearly twice the net worth of people who stayed single. In fact, married couples realized the equivalent of an extra four percent of income growth annually.

What accounts for this marked difference in wealth creation? Nothing jumps out in the data, but several things jump out at me as I think about my own marriage. First off, if both people in the marriage are working, they're likely making more than a single individual would make. But there are other considerations as well.

It's just common sense that two people live more efficiently together than separately. And two people who are intimately connected feel comfortable sharing more than do the average set of roommates. It's more reasonable to share large expenses like cars, homes, vacation rentals, and major appliances with the person we plan to be with for the lifetime of the purchase.

And then there is the motivation factor. Part of the juice behind marriage is the drive to set goals and achieve dreams with the help and support of a lifelong partner. We know that reaching goals is greatly helped by being accountable to a group rather than simply depending on yourself. Behavioral change programs such as Alcoholics Anonymous and WeightWatchers are successful largely because of the extra support that comes with being accountable to a group. Wealth-building is a slow, difficult process that requires judgment and perseverance. Having the accountability and support of a spouse surely adds to the success of the endeavor.

How about the added resources of marriage? Marriage brings a network of familial support in the form of parents, aunts, uncles, cousins, nieces, and nephews—all of whom may know something or someone who can help you along the way. As often as we may feel life would be easier without all that additional family, we have to accept that the larger network of folks who are invested in our marriage are also invested in our future and our goals.

As I think about my marriage, I realize that Martin and I co-created almost every major piece of intellectual property that we have used to generate income. Each of us looks at the world a little differently. When we bring those complementary outlooks together, we usually hit on a solution that is better than what we would have arrived at individually. That's the beauty of shared resources. None of us knows it all. A couple can create more and better together.

Martin and I have a little saying that there are no unreasonable goals, only unrealistic time frames. And we often remind ourselves and our staff that while the shortest distance between two points is a straight line, most often we tend to zigzag to our goals. Life just doesn't work as neatly as math. But one little observation I've made about being married to Martin is that when I am about to zig, sometimes Martin stops me before I zig too far. And when Martin is about to zag, I'm usually the one who can catch it and catch him. Perhaps that means that by working together toward common goals, we can forge a little straighter path for ourselves and get there a bit faster. That dynamic may contribute to our wealth-generating ability.

The recession of 2008, coupled with the responsibilities of college education for our kids and equipping the family with motor vehicles, insurance, and the like left me feeling as if our wealth-generating efforts were largely going flat. But where will I look to shore up our savings and regenerate lost income from investments that are no longer earning what they used to? To Martin, of course. To my marriage. And I know that two of us working together can certainly create a bigger impact than I could alone.

I'm also struck by how much more effective any wealth generation effort is when couples use the practices that work inside a viable business. Nobody creates and keeps wealth without a sound financial plan. Every couple should understand the basics of agreement, shared vision, budgeting, and planning. These tools make the marital business more successful.

So if lifelong marriage really, truly pays, it sure makes sense to invest in its health and wellbeing above just about anything else. That's an investment tip with a great likelihood of excellent returns over time!

Recession-Proof Your Marriage

How to stay bullish in
a bear marital environment.

We all felt it—the cold chill of the economic meltdown of 2008 now known as "The Great Recession." The slow freeze of the economy bit almost all of us in one way or another. Some put on their heavy winter wear and waited out the cold. Some were fully exposed and suffered frostbite. Recovery is late and long, leaving us with the grim understanding that we have indeed lived through a notable event in modern history.

All this has me thinking about those periods of cold in a marriage—those times when the relationship doesn't break under the pressure, but instead grows chilly and lifeless. A marital recession doesn't look that different to me from an economic one.

Webster's defines a recession as "the act or action of receding; a departing procession, a period of reduced economic activity." As I've looked back at the "recession" eras of my marriage, those thoughts seem to describe the experience to a "T."

The act or action of receding.

When we think in terms of economics we know that a drop in the Gross Domestic Product—the input vs. ouput value of the economy—lasting at least two quarters, signals the beginning of a recession. And isn't that the way it goes in marriage? You notice a period when each partner just doesn't seem to have the energy or desire to put into the marriage the kind of attention and energy that will produce real Domestic Output—comfort, warmth, excitement, concern. Your home life is on autopilot; you are going through the motions. There may not be any overt conflict in the house, but you just aren't making the little efforts you used to.

The warning signs are small. We forget to kiss hello and goodbye. We go to bed at different times or get involved in computers and newspapers and go silent at breakfast or in the evening. There isn't really anything to pin it on, except general life strain. Yet slowly the relationship cools.

A departing procession.

I like this because it reminds me of some of the most productive and satisfying times in my marriage, when Martin and I were deeply engaged in building our futures. We were visioning and planning. We were working on a budget or long-term goal. These sorts of activities drove our relationship forward in exciting ways. But life often has a way of intervening and taking our focus off each other. We're left on the sidelines of the parade, distracted by the issues of the day, and when we look up again, we can just make out the backs of the marching band three blocks ahead. We've fallen behind.

A period of reduced economic activity.

It's funny, but when I find myself caught in marital recession, it does feel much like a down economy. We're not investing in our relationship. We're not "spending" time with each other. This isn't the time when a romantic getaway sounds tempting. I'm more likely to long for a day in bed with the covers pulled over my head.

A marriage in crisis motivates many to act, to seek counseling, or make a big life change. Marital recession doesn't tend to incite these actions. After all, nothing big is really wrong. We've just lost our way.

And just like we reduce our spending to the level of necessity rather than luxury, we're tempted to just try to get by in our relationship without the extra, intentional effort.

Brrrr.

Most economists cite two ways to fight recession, and I believe they are not bad suggestions for recessions of the marital sort: *stimulus* and *investment*. Once you've recognized and agreed that your relationship is receding, try stimulating progress through some invigorating new goals and activities.

I was a distance runner for ten years. My daughter and I trained for many races together, and I always saw her as my perfect training partner. We were after all almost the same size, and our pace and stride were nearly equal. However, in an attempt to keep Martin motivated to exercise regularly and prepare myself for an upcoming marathon without my daughter in town, Martin and I began training together.

We were surprised by the spark this added to our relationship. We used the running time to have deeper conversations. We compared notes on progress toward our personal goals. It was a perfect time to ask each other for advice or support. And even though we weren't perfect pace partners, we discovered ways to overcome our differences. Martin often ran alongside me while rolling his bicycle until he had had enough, then would hop on his bike and act as my sag wagon. I'd have to say that this little marital "stimulus" was great for us.

In response to our son's approaching college tuition, we started feeling the pressure to get our financial house in order. We took a class on financial fundamentals and found that even that "stimulus" led to conversations, plans, and a feeling of "together for better."

We were never great at the tried-and-true advice to have a weekly date night. But we started purchasing season tickets to our theater, symphony, and other local arts organizations. We found that this bit of structure "stimulated" us to make a date for dinner before or after the show.

It may not seem like much, but these little nudges back into the relationship have a big influence on the quality of the marriage.

Really, investing in the relationship is key. As noted earlier, Martin and I are in that empty nest phase. I'm watching my friends navigate this transition with interest. Some are coming out from under their focus on parenting and realizing that they hadn't really been investing in each other. For a few, the marital bank account has emptied. Relationally bankrupt, they are splitting up and starting over. Some are making major investments in counseling, communication, and recommitment to a healthy relationship.

Some are enjoying this time as a second honeymoon of sorts— enjoying the payout from wise investing along the way.

Recovery is possible in marital recession, but it may be slow— just like the tentative economic recoveries our country tends to experience. My sincere wish is that we all feel the well-being that comes with a healthy economy—and enjoy a wonderful expansionary period in our relationships. Especially our marriages!

The Marital Return on Investment

Figuring the R.O.I. on a lifetime commitment.

I remember with such fondness the anticipation and preparation for my daughter's and son's weddings. They were both committed and ready to take this important step, but so many couples today aren't making the decision to officially wed, instead determining not to be bound by tradition. Many young adults experienced the pain and trauma of their parents' divorces and don't want to take a chance on an institution that has about a fifty percent chance of failure. At the same time, so many of our friends in the gay community have fought hard for their right to marry and are enjoying married life for themselves.

It makes me wonder. What do we expect to receive from marriage? When we make other major life decisions such as buying a house or deciding to move and begin a new job, we're pretty objective about weighing the risks and benefits. And in business, we are sticklers for determining ROI before adding staff or incurring debt. How might we calculate ROI on a marriage?

At nineteen, when I decided to tie the knot, I was convinced that this commitment would lead to a life of romance, deep happiness, safety, security, and a platform for achieving big dreams. I also wanted children and knew that commitment over the long-term would provide a healthy environment for raising and launching them. I didn't think much further than that. I knew

that I would be making an investment in fidelity, in supporting someone else's dreams and visions, in an extended family, in financial support, and homemaking support. Seemed like a good deal to me!

Looking back over four decades, has my marriage delivered a fair return? That's a way more complicated question to answer now! I will say yes. I have enjoyed some fabulous romance, many hours of happiness, support in times of stress and trouble, investment in so many dreams and aspirations, and most importantly, I've received the priceless gift of raising a beautiful family. But truthfully, I've experienced anger, doubt, frustration, fear, financial stress, and worry. In other words, it's complicated. And because married life is still life and not some elevated state, Martin and I have experienced life together fully and have shared the joys and bruises that life brings. Has our marital investment returned? I think so!

There are some very material and measurable benefits that a marriage can bring to a couple. The research is compelling and it runs the gamut from "soft assets" to cold hard cash. Here is a laundry list of financial, legal, health, and social advantages that married folks enjoy. The following points come from Kate Ashford, who wrote a very compelling article about the financial and legal benefits of a marriage license ("11 Things You Never Thought of When You Decided Not To Get Married," *Forbes*, September 2014):

- You'll qualify for an estate tax marital deduction. When one spouse dies, his or her estate passes to the surviving spouse, tax-free.

- You'll qualify for the gift tax marital deduction. As long as your spouse is a U.S. citizen, you can make tax-free gifts of any amount to him or her.

- You can roll over a deceased spouse's IRA to the surviving spouse's IRA. If your significant other dies with an IRA and you aren't married, you'll have to start taking distributions immediately, regardless of your age.

- You can contribute to a spousal IRA.

- You can receive survivor's benefits from a pension plan. If your spouse is lucky enough to have a pension, and they've elected to have survivor's benefits, you will continue receiving pension benefits after he or she dies.

- You can receive Social Security benefits. Spouses have the option of filing for a spousal benefit, which gives them the potential to collect up to fifty percent of the other spouse's benefit amount.

- You'll save on health insurance. Usually plans for one plus a spouse are cheaper than if you each have your own plan, even if it's an employer-sponsored plan.

- You have an advantage if your spouse is incapacitated. If your significant other is in a car crash, you may have more difficulty seeing him or her at a hospital if you aren't a blood relation or a legal spouse. And if a judge has to name someone to make healthcare or financial decisions on behalf of your partner, you may be overlooked in favor of a parent or sibling if you aren't married.

- You have more protection if your spouse dies. You have more legal rights. For instance, if your spouse is in a fatal accident, you can sue for wrongful death.

- You have a leg up when buying a home. Two spouses have a combined income and a legal reason to stay together—and mortgage lenders like that.

There's a lot there, and that is part of the reason why the gay community has fought so hard for legal marriage—there are legal and financial benefits.

Findings published by the National Bureau of Economic Research in 2014 revealed that, overall, being married makes people happier and more satisfied with their lives than those who remain single. And this is true especially during the most stressful periods, like midlife, when many people experience multiple demands of caring for aging parents, raising children, and financing college. The researchers noted that marital stability is highest among the most-educated and highest-earning couples. But the researchers suggested that the stability and security derived from stable marriages would also benefit those who are in the greatest distress.

Interestingly, these findings correlated in almost all areas of the globe, with a few notable exceptions: Latin America, South Asia, and sub-Saharan Africa.

And marital happiness tended to outlive the honeymoon period perhaps due to the wonderful long-term returns of friendship over time. I remember having lunch with a confirmed bachelor many years ago, who shared an insight I've never forgotten. He said his biggest motivator for considering marriage was the loss he would experience from having no one with whom to share a history if he opted out of the commitment. He said, "I want someone who can say, 'Remember when …?'" By the way, this gentleman is now happily married and making those memories!

That friendship and history are so valuable. Martin and I have taken our children to the playground where my friend and I were once bombarded by persimmons thrown by none other than my darling husband. I was five at the time! We have a little history!

Can marriage make you healthier? This idea was researched back in the 1850s by William Farr, who found correlations between better health and the married couples he studied in France. Updated studies prove more nuanced. Research coming out of the Ohio State University College of Medicine by the duo Ronald Glaser and Jan Kiecolt-Glaser (spouses, by the way) suggests that the health advantage in married couples was not present in stressed and unhappy marriages, which seemed to impede immune response. So receiving a return on your health investment correlates directly to the health of your marriage.

There is also some solid research that wealth is easier to build and maintain in marriage, making a sort of economic argument for marital ROI. (More on this in the chapter, "Recession-Proof Your Marriage").

Most mainstream religious organizations point out all sorts of studies in support of the institution and its benefits to the individual and even to society as a whole. But each of us has a unique story around choosing to be married or choosing to be single, and I'm sure I would have a heap of coals dropped on my head by happy, healthy, wealthy single friends who have weighed the benefits and risks of marrying and have determined that for them, the return was simply not there.

One thing stands out for me as I weigh the research: marriage is still a revered and important institution to our culture that receives much respect and many benefits, both legal and cultural. It is still very much a sought-after institution and extends well beyond a religious ceremony to a civil action. No wonder folks fight for the right to choose it. No wonder I chose it. And now I have the responsibility to ensure that I gain the return on my investment.

Production and Operations/Resource Management

Getting it Done

Tools to enhance productivity at home.

*I*n the workplace, we're all at home with the subject of productivity. No matter what business you are in, you are quite simply producing something—a product or service upon which others place a tangible value and pay a specific price to receive. Productivity is measurable, and most employees know with some specificity how productive they are expected to be to remain employed in the job. Productive employees produce profits or other positive business outcomes. Unproductive employees get the boot.

This clarity could be of real benefit when it comes to getting things done at home. I don't believe I've ever seen productivity as a measure of value in the marriage partnership, and I know there isn't a measure of output that exists when it comes to the business of life. Yet life is work! There's a lot to be done. And every family has some measure of productivity relative to producing a desired lifestyle at home. If you want clean clothes, fed kids, a house without a leaky roof, you've got work to produce.

This messy gray area leads to all kinds of struggle when couples navigate the duties related to making a home. Martin and I have had our fair share of fights around the broken thing that just never has gotten fixed or the bill that was supposed to be paid. And these sorts of disagreements can get ugly. At home, we don't always employ the best skills for communicating in order to get things done. We ask—again and again—we complain, we accuse, or worst of all, we nag. None of these techniques goes over too well at work. Why do we think it will get us somewhere at home?

The workplace, after all, is all about pulling together to get things done—productivity by definition. I open a job order and ask my team to work together to complete the task at hand, on deadline, within budget—oh, and brilliantly. As principal of the firm, I think the majority of my interactions with our staff center around my asking them for something. Why am I able to manage all these requests without resorting to nagging or broken-record-reminding in order to get things done cooperatively? I've certainly had situations where my co-workers promised to do something for me and then appeared to waffle and waver, putting off the request and responding in vague ways. But somehow the way we communicate in the office seems to quell the nag—not bring it out.

I remember being coached around the idea of requests and agreements. Our coach told us that most of the frustration happens when "You don't fulfill a request I didn't make." Meaning that we often think we have asked for something but haven't really done so in a way that makes it clear that we have a request and an agreement between us. Our team learned to use the language, "I have a request" (can't get much clearer). Now that is just the beginning. The requestee should then respond with their agreement, questions, clarifications, or concerns. Still, an agreement isn't complete until the two parties decide on a proper time for the action and on a way to close the loop with each other, or confirm that the action has been completed to the best of the responder's understanding.

By the way, this works like a charm. It puts equal responsibility on both parties. The requester has to be perfectly clear, answer questions and concerns, and agree to certain terms and conditions—such as a time frame. The requestee has to respond with respect and truth of intention and has the responsibility to negotiate the time frame and ask for clarity or even motives.

This isn't easy. And Lord knows it is so easy just to nag at home. We feel very safe with our mates; we entered a covenant agreement to take care of one another's needs. It is so frustrating to try to take care of the business of life with a partner who seems less than responsive to your needs. Likewise, it is really a pain to be goaded into submission. Doesn't he or she know that you intend to do this—just on your terms?

That safety net we weave around our intimate relationships can create a comfy blanket from which we revert to childish habits or lazy behavior. But the truth is, these relationships are fragile. That very sort of unconscious behavior can knock holes in the safety net and leave us wounded and tempted to move on. I think one of the reasons that bringing some of my work habits home has been helpful is because they simply force thoughtful and pre-meditated behavior and communication. I usually think before I act or blurt or nag at work because I more readily see the danger associated if I don't. Likewise, making a point to be more thought-ful at home is the key to creating happiness.

Michael Theriault, a contributor to Forbes Online Journal, pro-vides some tips for upping productivity in the workplace. ("If You Want More Productive Employees, Learn How to Get Out Of Their Way," February 2014). I think they work well at home too.

Offer a global view, not limited information.

At work, I know that I can't really dictate how someone does the job, but I can offer the big picture and clarity on my expecta-tions. For example, the request "Take out the trash" is direct, but there are actually a lot of ways to "take out the trash": gather everything into one big bag then take it out to the street. Take all the garbage to the garbage can, but leave it on the porch for someone else to deliver to the street. Take out the garbage in the kitchen only. Take out the garbage once a week, daily, hourly. A talk about the big picture around trash removal is called for!

Share goals and objectives, not instructions.

Shall I repeat the first thought from above about not dictating how the job is done? Micromanagement is a productivity killer in the workplace—and a marriage killer at home. If I ask you to fold the clothes or fill the dishwasher, I don't get to complain about your technique for rolling socks. I do get to share my objectives such as, folding clothes means folding them in a way that won't make them wrinkled. Or filling the dishwasher means prepping the dishes in such a way that they are actually clean after dishwashing.

Provide support and facilitation, not barriers.

Sometimes I ask Martin to take care of something at home, but I don't even consider providing him with some of the kinds of support that I automatically give my staff when I make a request of them. Often I help pave the way for my employees by offering resources, knowledge, options, and advice. If I prepped Martin the way I do my staff, I bet he'd be able to get the job done better, and more easily.

Finally, give freedom to act, not permission to act.

We know that dictating to a spouse is a real marriage killer, but let's face it, it can be easy to get a little too involved in every little decision. It can also be tempting to "check-in" a bit too often about the task at hand. At work, Theirolt suggests establishing a simple update mechanism to keep everyone on the same page with an opportunity to raise a red flag or get things back on track. One of my friends has been having a little weekly "business meeting" with her spouse to check on progress, make some agreements, and generally keep stuff on track. Martin and I use the Covey planning system and often use our weekly planning as a time for checking in and staying on track with home work.

I'd like to throw in another bit of advice gained through experience: don't use email or text to get to the bottom of a request situation gone wrong. It is just too easy to "go there" in writing, or ignore the message if you are on the receiving end. I've just about stopped using email for anything but affirmation and confirmation of what we've discussed face-to-face if at all possible. I just don't think we have a handle on how to communicate well and clearly via the airwaves. And I'm embarrassed by my inability to really absorb communication presented on a screen. My lizard brain just hasn't gotten there yet.

It may not be romantic, but getting things done is a big part of married life. Productivity is a good thing. And getting things done without conflict is a real life enhancer.

Your Marital Hours of Operation

Open 24/7 or standard business hours? It's a good idea to think about when you are open for business—and when business is closed!

*O*h, what a complicated age we live in. The line between work and home life is blurry at best, and in many cases has ceased to exist altogether. That old average work day of eight hours from 9:00 to 5:00 is fading, replaced by the brave new virtual world, where we can all work from home and do business with anyone around the globe. This all means that we can work whenever and wherever we want to: it sounds good on the face of it. The downside, however, is the tendency to never really turn off work-mode and tune in to our significant other or family—let alone ourselves.

A mountain of research has established our growing addiction to our cell phones—some studies suggesting that we check our phones an average of nine times an hour! The incessant buzzing and chirping sends us drooling like Pavlov's dogs to respond to, in the words of Stephen Covey, the urgent rather than the important.

Work–life balance is a hot topic of conversation. Employers are adapting to this 24/7 work world by being more flexible—understanding that people blend their private to-dos into their office hours and, in exchange, work from home on nights and weekends.

So what are the formal business hours of operation anymore? At Thoma Thoma, we are formally open from 8:30 to 5:00 or 5:30. But come by at 7:00 a.m. (or 7:00 p.m., for that matter) and you'll likely find someone working away at their computer. And our team is never surprised to receive email from my husband sent at 5:00 a.m.

The new world order of hybridized work and always-on technology has blurred the boundaries between work and home life. As a result, many people report they find themselves working all the time.

It begs the question, how much time is required to really nurture a marriage? Decades of experience have taught me that focused, quality time between spouses is an absolute requirement for marital health. Perhaps one of the reasons so many marriages don't make it is because over time, couples lose their motivation to put in the hours necessary to nurture their relationships.

In my own marriage, raising kids, working, volunteering, and trying to keep the house and yard from falling apart can seriously erode the hours Martin and I have available to date and pay attention to each other like we did when we were first married. Consider the hours you once put in talking online or on the phone and doing things together (not to mention all the hours spent in bed!) when you were first in love and living together.

Because Martin and I are empty-nested now, we have the opportunity to reconnect and rekindle that kind of quality time. I looked around to see if I could get some answers to just how many hours one needed to spend "at relationship."

Dr. Willard Harley, a renowned marriage counselor and author of the book, *His Needs, Her Needs: Building an Affair-Proof Marriage*, has some answers for us. On his website, marriagebuilders.com, Harley provides a Policy of Undivided Attention for couples. Based on his experience working with couples the policy reads: *Give your spouse your undivided attention a minimum of fifteen hours each week, using the time to meet the emotional needs of affection, sexual fulfillment, intimate conversation, and recreational companionship.*

Wow. That's a lot of time, isn't it? Dr. Harley adds that this is for healthy, stable marriages. He recommends more time for couples in crisis. His definition of *undivided attention* is quite strict—alone without kids, friends, or relatives. And not engaged in fighting or working.

Now, Martin and I spend a great deal of time in each other's physical presence. We sit across from one another at work, after all. But when I began to actually add up the time we spend alone really connecting in conversation that is not business or business-of-life related, I'm embarrassed at how few hours I can count.

It gets even more complicated than that. I was visiting about this with a newly remarried friend. When I mentioned that I was thinking about marital hours of operation, she made a terrific point.

"Yeah," she said. "The other night, I was just settling down on the couch with a good book, and my husband stretched out and put his feet in my lap. He was open for business. I was not!"

Couples are not always in sync about when they come together to connect and when each partner needs to turn around that OPEN FOR BUSINESS sign and have some personal time and space.

My daughter, when she was newly engaged, noted that her man often wanted to "relax" together. In her childhood, relaxing meant being together in the same room, but perhaps everyone was doing their own thing. This isn't what her partner means. He is actually referring to undivided attention time. Relaxing meant closed for business to her and open for business to him.

Creating this kind of space clearly requires a deep conversation—and some negotiation. Martin and I try to go on a real date about once a week. We plan these so they don't get to be routine. And frankly, it's harder than we thought it would be. We're creating some new things to come together around, such as spending time together in our new community garden plot.

We've always made a point of celebrating anniversaries in a big way and getting away on weekends; so planning trips around anniversaries seems like a good way to create that quality time we're looking for. Years of early morning training runs during my marathon days have both of us conditioned to jump out of bed at the crack of dawn on the weekends, but we're trying to slow that morning time down and focus on each other rather than meeting mileage goals.

We have a way to go to get fifteen solid hours of marital operation, but we're getting there. And the conversation, as well as the extra effort, has certainly had a positive effect on our relationship.

The Seven Habits of Effective Family Management

A planner's approach to time and life management.

A year or so after launching our business, I hit a wall. I was overworked, overwhelmed—and frankly, just over it. Martin and I were running our business from our home and raising our young daughter with basically no child care. It seemed as if we had no real boundaries between work and home life. I was multi-tasking my way through each day—working on the computer while parenting, cooking during business meetings with Martin. I was meeting deadlines for sure—but not meeting many personal goals.

And then I found a book that I refer to as the second most influential read of my life, second only to the Bible (I'm actually serious here!): Stephen Covey's *The 7 Habits of Highly Effective People*. Covey posits that effective people are principle-driven and achieve great personal effectiveness through the development of habits of character. Covey introduced a time management system consistent with these habits that I put into practice and quite frankly changed my life for the better.

Two aspects of the Covey time-management method were particularly good for me. One is the understanding that if I manage my world by a list, everything has about the same priority, so over time I become motivated by what has become most urgent verses what is most important to me.

The second aspect of this method is that it involves planning around all the different roles we play in life. I am not just a business person, or a homemaker. I'm mother, wife, manager, volunteer, writer, performer. Making space to set goals and create time for these roles over the course of a week, month, or year means that I can move all aspects of my life forward and not give over to sacrificing my personal goals for my work demands.

Martin and I began Covey planning every week and have kept it up for more than thirty years. And I brought it into Thoma several years ago, requiring my staff to adopt a time-management system and training them in Covey planning. This common understanding of the system has been helpful. If someone is struggling to meet multiple deadlines and manage multiple jobs—a daily reality in a marketing firm—we can look at their week and use the Covey tools to create a solution.

Lately we've been working on some global goals aimed at improving the business. These are just the sorts of "to dos" that are often pushed aside to address the "urgent" deadlines of the daily work. But a simple prompt to "Covey" the work is usually enough for our staff to slow down and schedule time to work on the big picture—even mapping the work out over weeks or an entire quarter.

I introduced *The 7 Habits* and the time-management system to my kids around middle school. This is likely the first time children are given a planner for school work. The *7 Habits* book for teens written by Covey's son is quite good for children this age. My daughter also uses this method to this day, and my son, while not as close an adherent, understands the value of working ahead and melding small and large goals into each day to achieve life balance.

Martin and I have had a firsthand experience of using two different planning tools. For a few years, Martin adopted a weekly and daily planner that was really excellent for the workplace. The planner allowed for detailed thought and scheduling around almost any work situation. But it didn't account for the rest of life.

You know those agreements that you make to your partner around say, fixing the broken doorknob or getting the shower regrouted? During the years when Martin was using the work planner rather than the Covey method, those types of "to do's" never made it into his week. Personal and home goals began to make their way to a long list and were addressed when they became a crisis. And yes, that crisis just might have been me blowing a gasket over all the pesky little things we had agreed to do that weren't being done.

Martin switched back to the Covey method after a couple of years, and everything has gone so much smoother. There is a place in this system for noting those little "to do's" and addressing them. I know Martin hasn't forgotten his home tasks and goals. And he knows that I'll address mine. When we want to plan a big trip or develop a budget for the new year, we'll often say, "Let's Covey that." And without so much fuss or last-minute stress, things get done. And since both of us do our weekly planning on Sunday evenings, we often use that time to have a bit of a meeting about our week and coordinate together.

I believe this time-management system is one that you can take into your family and really see results with. My staff members often report that as they are learning the system, they may still be struggling to schedule their work tasks, but they are making time for the important things in life beyond work. I call that success. Using the tools as a family and teaching the method to your young teens can bring you together and create room for dialog and planning—pre-empting some of the last-minute scramble that leads to so many blow-ups. This is really a great tool to give to your children.

So if you haven't read it before, purchase the book and then check out the resources available to assist with Covey planning. You may also see that you can be more effective at work and at home.

Leadership and
Human Resources

Who's the Boss in Your Family?

Match strengths and abilities to
common household tasks, the same
way you assign duties at work.

*M*ost businesses create an organizational chart. They break the work down into areas of responsibility and define them further by required skill sets and accompanying tasks. Applicants are screened for their experience, training, and aptitude before they are assigned to the jobs. Doing so makes the business run better.

But does this happen at home? Not often.

Answer these questions: who's the CEO in your family? And who's the CFO?

Applying a bit of management discipline to your home life can open new possibilities. Consider the skills and aptitudes required by real life and match them to the unique abilities each of you brings to the relationship.

Take the CEO, for example. The primary role of the CEO at work is holding the vision and setting strategy, not "being the boss," as is generally assumed. When I think about the role of home CEO, I ask myself, who in this family tends to carry the vision for the future and see the big picture? That would be me.

As CEO, I am responsible for planning the future. What does summer look like for the family as a whole and for each child? Where would we like to travel? Are we on track to complete that

kitchen renovation? What goals must we reach in order to make the whole system, as well as each individual, better?

On the other hand, Martin is the best fit for CFO, so he manages all things financial. Does he get to decide what we purchase? No. That would be the purchasing agent—me. He's responsible for creating the annual budget, paying the bills, determining the best plan for college or retirement savings, and monitoring those investments.

COO? Well, when it comes to operating the household, we break it up into inside (me) and outside (him). These choices aren't about traditional roles. These are about what each of us does best. This became really clear when we had very young children. Martin can fall asleep anywhere, anytime, in an instant. If I am awakened in the night, I cannot go back to sleep. Guess who managed the bulk of the nighttime care duties in our house?

On top of that, I'm blessed (or cursed, depending on how you look at it) with a head of curls that would make Orphan Annie jealous. The only approach to hair care is to wash it and let it be. Our daughter, Claire, has beautiful, wavy black hair. It requires more than mere maintenance; it calls for artistry! Martin took on the role of coiffeur, mastering the French braid and other lovely updos. And because we both hate housework, we outsource.

What roles do you play in your family life? Are you doing that job because you have the right aptitude and skill, or are you doing it because "that's how it was done in my family" or "it's a woman's job"?

Do you find yourself angry and annoyed at your partner each time you perform a certain task? Chances are you aren't made for the job. If both of you hate it, pay someone else to do it, even if you have to tighten up elsewhere. Martin and I cut back on dinners out, double lattes, and manicures in order to pay for some help in the home and kitchen. Now we have clean clothes, bathed dogs, food in the 'fridge, and a chance to take a nap on Saturday afternoons.

You might find that neither of you is great at keeping the checkbook balanced and the bills paid on time. These processes can be automated with a little investment in technology. That's what happens at work, right? Making those little investments can pay off big when you raise your credit score and lower your blood pressure.

By the way, the two of you may not be the only "staffers" at home, so consider applying the discipline of delegation and job descriptions to your kids. My daughter was my personal assistant during high school. She paid for her car insurance by working it off ten to twelve hours a week.

If outsourcing those irksome tasks or investing in household technology (Roomba, anyone?) saves you conflict and stress, you have managed your budget wisely.

Sometime soon over coffee or wine, work with your partner to identify all the jobs required to run the "business of life" for your family. Map these jobs into roles on your "org chart." Then match family members to the positions and tasks that leverage their strengths and native abilities. At home—as in business—becoming more intentional about this process can foster a more peaceable kingdom.

Give Your Relationship an Annual Review

You do it for your business, so why not for your home life? Assess your accomplishments and set new goals now.

At the beginning of each new calendar year, the managers at our firm are engaged in a tradition as old as business—the annual review. We've struggled with this process over the years, finding it oppressive and somehow Machiavellian to spend an hour getting very clear with our employees about their performance on the job when they should know exactly how they stand in relation to their job performance throughout the year. Annual reviews can feel like big, bad surprises. I've never been convinced that "grading" an employee at the start or end of each calendar year is motivating or helpful.

Instead, we've tried to adopt a quarterly sit-down for our staff that enables managers to give insight into how the employee's behavior is jibing with our core values, how they are performing in terms of their job accountabilities, and how they might improve. Or if all is well, it's a time to celebrate their contribution.

Over time, our annual reviews have become more of an "annual plan" for the coming year. What does the employee hope to accomplish? Where would he/she like to grow or stretch? What does he/she need to work on to become a better cultural or professional fit? These types of annual conversations can inspire and motivate. And no one knows better than I do, because Martin and I have been doing an annual "marital" review every year for just about all of our married lives.

It began years ago on one of those gray, cold January snow days that are perfect at locking up traffic and closing schools and business in the South. I remember the two of us getting out some notebook paper and spending a good part of a wintry day just free-forming everything we wanted for ourselves and our marriage in the coming year. We just spit our ideas out and wrote them down. They naturally categorized themselves into dreams about health, wealth, travel, home, family life, spiritual life, and business. At the end of our musings, Martin just tore out the pages and put them in a file that we conveniently forgot until the next year when he found them again in a fit of New Year's organizing.

Looking at them, we were stunned! We had accomplished almost everything we set out to do. We had totally forgotten that we wrote we wanted a piano, and by golly, there was one in our living room! We had been asked to babysit a Mason & Hamlin baby grand for some folks who were between houses. We could never have afforded to purchase one during that year, but we had one just the same!

Martin looked at me and grinned! We have to do this again this year, he said. And so we did. We made our plans, spit out some big dreams, then we put them in the file and forgot them. But according to research, we never really forgot them, we just let them sink into our conscious and subconscious minds where, in the background, they were being considered and held and worked on until they bubbled up into our reality. Some folks call it manifesting. And others just like to think that goals are the road map to obtainment. Whatever you may believe, the great majority of anything we wrote down each year came to pass. And it was gratifying to watch it all unfold.

These reviews represent some of the most productive and meaningful conversations we have. Unlike the traditional employee review, we don't review each other. Rather, each of us sticks to discussion and evaluation of our own experiences. We just listen to the other—especially when making observations about problems or failures.

Here is the outline of our annual review meeting held each January:

A Review of the Past Year

- Look over the notes from the last review and annual goal-setting exercise:

    * What did you accomplish personally, and as a couple, that you are proud of?

    * What frustrated you?

    * Where do you think you could improve?

A Look at the Year Ahead

- What do you want to accomplish?

- How will you work together to accomplish this plan?

- Just as we would do at the office, we break our look ahead into categories—such as personal growth, health and wellness, children, finances, and vacation.

Budget Review and Resetting

- As with businesses, how you deploy your financial resources is a reflection of your values, principles, and mission.

- Now is the time to ensure that your money and your principles remain in alignment.

This meeting is also a great time to look over your relationship's mission statement or create one if you haven't done it before.

One practice is an absolute must. Regardless of whether you'll refer back to your plans and statements, you **must** write them down. **Writing** your goals and objectives brings them from the world of thought into the physical world—the first, necessary step in seeing them manifest in your actual life.

Business guru Peter Drucker said, "Plans are only good intentions unless they immediately degenerate into hard work." We might paraphrase and say, "A goal is but a wish unless you write it down and first bring it into the world."

We've noticed that our planning was a sort of bellwether for our personal and marital well-being. The Great Recession of 2008 delivered a really tough year to many businesses and families. Years like this can create an environment of stress and anger— not the best frame of mind for the annual review. Other years, when we got busy and failed to make an annual plan, were the challenging ones when we found ourselves mired in a complicated business situation or feeling disconnected as mates. Recognizing that we needed some way to come together, process a tough year, and move beyond it to motivate us for annual planning, Martin and I hit on a little exercise that was helpful, and it might work for you:

Individually, write down your disappointments, grievances, regrets. Let yourself go. Really get into this. You can use all the expletives, nasty descriptors, and unfair advantages you need to express yourself. Take your time and get it all down.

Now fold that paper up, take those notes to the nearest flame (fireplace, outdoor grill, campfire). Look at each other and say, "This was real. These feelings were valid. I'm releasing them, and I'm releasing our relationship from them." Then burn those suckers up! It's over. It's a new year. Time to commit to moving on.

Now work on that annual review in this refreshed frame of mind. And see what happens! (Yep, we've done this one more than once and it was a pretty awesome exercise.)

We're not alone in believing that this age-old business tradition should become de rigueur for couples. Elizabeth Bernstein writes in the *Wall Street Journal* that a growing number of therapists and relationship researchers recommend that couples complete some sort of performance evaluation periodically ("A Performance Review May be Good For Your Marriage," Oct. 5, 2015). She cites that research shows regular checkups improve relationships. In a study published in September 2014 in the *Journal of Consulting and Clinical Psychology*, couples were given questionnaires asking them to assess the strengths and weaknesses in their relationship. Half the couples then saw therapists for a checkup of two sessions to go over the evaluation while the other half were told they were on a waiting list and didn't discuss the assessments. Couples who had performed the evaluations saw significant improvements in their partner, and the couples that reported the most problems prior to the checkups saw the most improvement.

The *Wall Street Journal* published its own Performance Review sourced from the James Cordova Center for Couples and Family Research, Clark University (http://www.wsj.com/media/2015-marriage-review2.pdf). Here it is below:

1. What positive praise do you have for your marriage?

2. Rate the following strengths in your marriage on a scale of 1 to 5.

- We are good friends.

- Our marriage is a high priority for both of us.

- We chat, touch base, or check in regularly about what's going on in our separate day-to-day lives.

- We laugh or smile together.

- We are a good team when it comes to parenting.

3. Rate the following concerning factors about your marriage on a scale of 1 to 5.

- We don't regularly spend enough quality time together.

- We don't clearly and effectively communicate our wants and needs to each other.

- We are unhappy with our sex life.

- We tend to disagree more than agree when it comes to money issues.

- Work stress can be an issue for us.

4. Identify one thing in your marriage you would like to improve. (Example: Talk more over dinner.)

5. List the ways you intend to meet your objective and how you will measure your success. Make a date to review the outcome.

6. Sign off with a positive goal. (Example: "Susan, I aim to empathize with and understand you. Love, Steve.")

I really like the looks of the review. It's quick and easy but great fodder for a productive conversation.

Divorce mediator Sam Margulies writes for *Psychology Today* that he's been struck by the obliviousness of couples to their marital health ("The Annual Marital Performance Review," February 10, 2010). He writes, "It takes a long time for a marriage to erode to the point that the couple is held together only by inertia and fear of the consequences of separation. Presumably, two people of reasonable intelligence and good faith would have some awareness of what was happening and would act in concert to remedy the problems of the marriage before it reaches the irretrievable tipping point. But in reality this seldom seems to happen."

Margulies offers this review for couples to consider:

In this review each spouse is asked to grade the other's performance by responding to a five-point scale from strongly agree to strongly disagree. The review consists of a series of questions, each one premised by *In the past year how have I performed on the following behaviors?*

Strongly agree	1
Agree	2
Not sure	3
Disagree	4
Strongly disagree	5

Affection

- I have given you the physical affection that you need.
  1 2 3 4 5

- I have been sensitive to your sexual needs. 1 2 3 4 5

- I have provided you with the emotional affirmation you need. 1 2 3 4 5

- I have been supportive when you were stressed and troubled. 1 2 3 4 5

- I have spent as much time with you as you needed.
  1 2 3 4 5

Communication

- I have listened well when you were telling me something that was important to you. 1 2 3 4 5

- When we disagreed on something I was respectful of you and willingly engaged until we resolved the issue. 1 2 3 4 5

- During the year you felt comfortable raising difficult issues with me and did not feel you had to bury important issues. 1 2 3 4 5

- I have been transparent with you about my feelings so you did not have to guess about them. 1 2 3 4 5

- Together we have successfully resolved the important issues on which we disagreed. 1 2 3 4 5

- On most days I have been reasonably cheerful. 1 2 3 4 5

Money

- I have been a good provider for the family this year. 1 2 3 4 5

- I have responsibly marshaled and preserved the resources of the family. 1 2 3 4 5

- I have consulted with you in good faith regarding major expenditures of money. 1 2 3 4 5

Household

- I have done my fair share of housework this year. 1 2 3 4 5

Parenting

- I have done my fair share of childcare and parenting this year. 1 2 3 4 5

- You approve of my approach to parenting and discipline. 1 2 3 4 5

- I spend enough time with the children. 1 2 3 4 5

- I spend too much time with the children and not enough time with you. 1 2 3 4 5

Again, there is a lot of here to drive a conversation, but counselors are quick to point out that couples should not use this time for blame and criticism. Instead this should be an opportunity to be frank and then strategize solutions.

Martin and I tried an evaluation from Michele Lisenbury Christensen at this year's marital review. While it was helpful, we ended up going back to our tried-and-true brainstorming and things went better. I think we enjoyed the creativity and positivity of looking ahead as a way of keeping us solutions-oriented rather than blaming or complaining.

We filled several sheets of notebook paper, and then filed it away—ready for next year and grateful for another opportunity to get it better.

The One-Minute Manager for Home and Family

Learn to give effective feedback
in less than sixty seconds.

Every few years, I pull a dog-eared little book off my shelf at work and reread a business classic, *The One Minute Manager*. Published in the early '80s, this book lays out a simple, clear process for giving employee feedback and inspiring appropriate behavior based on the premise that folks work harder when they feel good about themselves. And in order to feel good about themselves and their work, they need super-clear goals and expectations, super-responsive feedback, and some super-positive strokes from someone who truly cares about them.

At Thoma Thoma, we are currently in the process of refining the roles of each staff member and providing them with some measureable ways to chart their success. So a good refresh on this book is in order. And it has prompted me to think back to the days when I had young children. One Minute Management sure would have been a lifesaver then! As I review the techniques, I'm sure that any family with young children would benefit from a quick, clear method for dealing with the junior partners in the family.

Back in the days of toddlers and sleep deprivation, Martin and I had a pretty good system for managing the behavior of our little ones, and it paralleled the One Minute Manager very closely.

First, a One Minute Manager sets clear, simple goals with each employee that fit on one page and can be read in one minute. The goal might be to solve problems in distribution, which will maximize volume and minimize waste. Then there might be a measurable outcome. Another example might be to reduce error followed by a dollar-value ceiling for mistakes.

When our kids were young, each had a poster on the fridge with just such goals. They were simple, short, and clear as it gets. *Do not bite anyone. No yelling inside the house. Eat when you are hungry and stop when you are full. When you are in a store, enjoy with your eyes instead of your hands.*

We never had more than five goals for each child, and they were age appropriate. Later in life a goal might read: *Drive with no more than two other friends in the car.*

Before we went into a store, or got into the car, or had a friend over, we took a moment to review the goals that pertained to the situation. If we were shopping, for instance, outside the store, I would remind my daughter that she was to enjoy with her eyes only.

The second step in the One Minute Manager process is to find ways to catch employees doing well and to praise them. Let them know when they are on track. This totally worked for me when it came to the kids.

Back to the store with my daughter. As we walked through the store, I would say things to her like, "Wow, look at you using your eyes! Isn't this fun! See the pretty colors your eyes can see in here? Good job not touching or breaking!"

It sounds corny, but ninety percent of the time, it worked so beautifully that when we left she might get a little piece of candy for a reward. Sometimes she just got a big hug and kiss and my goofy celebration dance for how well she did in the store.

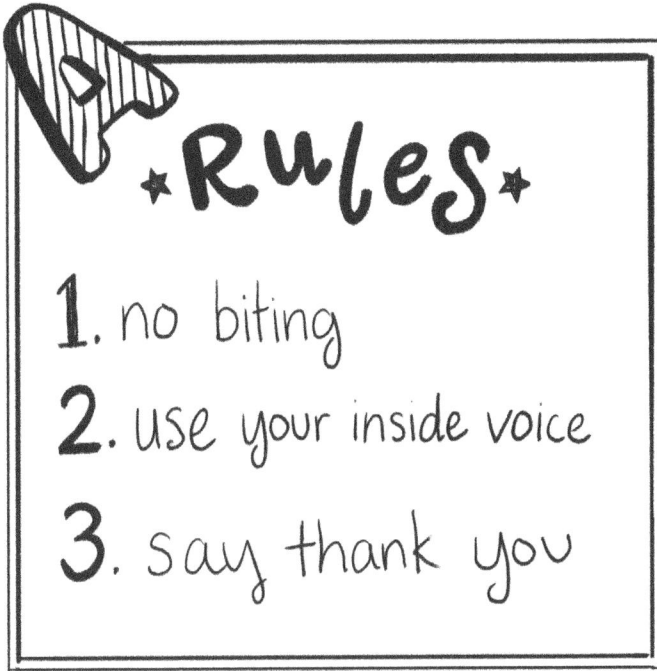

★Rules★

1. no biting

2. use your inside voice

3. say thank you

Now what about when those little teammates don't behave so well and need a reprimand? Well, a One Minute reprimand is swift, clearly communicates what the employee did wrong, and tells how it made the manager feel.

I do remember vividly the day my daughter decided to throw a fit in a store at the mall. She knew the goal; we went over that before we went in. So I picked her up around the middle, feet first, and carried her out to the car. I left stuff on the floor of the store. No kidding.

When we got home, I told her in no uncertain terms how it was *not* any fun to be at the store with her when she misbehaved and that she would have a time out. I told her that any time she behaved like that in the store, a hasty exit followed by time out would be what she could expect.

But One Minute Managers aren't done. They let the employee know that they care for them as a person; they just don't care for the behavior or mistake. They let them know that they still believe in them.

And that's how I ended my little management project. I told Claire that I knew that she could behave well in stores, and that we would have more fun store adventures in the future when she brought her good behavior into the store.

I have to say that we depended heavily on our little set of five rules (or goals for behavior) and quick, clear reprimands with no arguing when we were raising children. Those children are grown now—and they turned out fine! I can't say it was due to my management style, but I can say my management style worked to make me feel more effective as a parent. What parent couldn't use that reinforcement? I may just pop that little book inside the gift box of the next expectant parent I know along with a soft, cuddly blanket. Not a bad gift!

What if "Wife" were a Job Title?

Position available: Wife. Starts immediately.

A recent project updating our company's job descriptions has me thinking about the title I hold called "Wife." After all, anyone who has done it will tell you, being married is a job! What if I were charged with creating a job description for this role and posting it at Monster.com or Indeed.com and elsewhere? What might that look like? Let's see:

Job Title:

Life Mate, Manager of Spousal Relationships for Family Unit.

Sounds impressive. But obviously a small enterprise and not a Fortune 500 play.

Position Posting:

Family unit seeks female senior executive for full-time (we're talking *all the time*) development of intimate relationships, nurture, care, and feeding of mate and offspring. This exciting and creative venture seeks to execute a multigenerational strategy of developing the highest possible quality of life through shared resources and support. The very life and happiness of team members will be the responsibility of the Life Mate, who will leverage her skills in communication and negotiation to ensure the health of the primary couple relationship and the proper development of junior staff.

LIFE MATE
Manager of Spousal Relations

The Life Mate must pledge her permanent fidelity to the enterprise and must be willing to assign all assets and available resources to the job.

Wow ... this sounds like hard work! I hope it pays well.

Responsibilities include:

- Willingness to relocate anywhere and everywhere that opportunity may take the business unit.

- Feeding, clothing, housing, and primary care of the company and its staff.

- Development and coordination of schedules that accommodate all parties.

- Continuous guidance, mentoring, development, discipline, and management of junior staff.

Resources Provided:

None. All resources are the responsibility of the job holder.

Termination Conditions:

This is a right-to-work state, meaning that the job holder may be asked to leave at any time with or without cause.

Qualifications:

- No experience required, just the desire to hold the position.

- No experience required with management or mentoring of junior staff.

- No experience required with setting or keeping budgets.

- No experience required in managing households or maintaining property.

- No prior experience in the bedroom necessary, but good skills are appreciated!

Benefits:

Although vacation, health insurance, life insurance, and other basic benefits are the responsibility of the job holder, certain tangible and intangible benefits accrue:

* Research indicates that people employed in this position may live longer than their single counterparts.

* Research indicates that for many people, successful engagement in the enterprise yields high levels of life satisfaction.

Would you take this job? Better yet, are you qualified? Clearly there are no true qualifications necessary, yet the job itself may be the most complicated position you'll ever hold. In business there is typically a well-defined manner in which to prepare yourself for a job with such daunting responsibilities.

Once again, the business world can teach some relationship skills.

The first requirement of preparing for a complex job is **education**. There are amazing resources on relationships, marriage, and family for any willing candidate to tap. One of the most instructive books I've read on marriage and relationship is

Harville Hendrix's *Getting the Love You Want* (http://www.har-villehendrix.com/). Hendrix presents his theory of Imago Relationship Therapy and practical, actionable advice for couples.

The best resource I've ever read for family dynamics and developing a healthy family culture is the late Virginia Satir's *The New Peoplemaking*. Satir was a pioneer in family counseling. This one book offers a master's degree in organizational development for the family.

J. Zink is an author and lecturer who taught Martin and me the method we used for disciplining our young children. His system: have no more than five rules at a time. Create simple, clear rewards and consequences for following or breaking those rules. Post them on the fridge, review them daily with your kids, and reward and enforce religiously. We didn't try to make it up as we went along. We didn't just do what our parents did. We researched a method that made sense and felt right for us; then we learned it and followed it. It worked! My kids still talk about how simple and effective this system was in guiding their development.

Then there is **training**. You are never really expected to land at a desk and just start working without some job training. Why shouldn't the same be true of marriage? For instance, how many relationships have failed because the mates were woefully untrained in household finances? We know financial stress is a huge risk issue for relationships. Where's the M.B.A.—Marriage Business and Administration?

Communications is another area that all of us need some real coaching in. Why don't we make that training a priority? There is a good assessment tool on what we call emotional intelligence at TalentSmart.com, that ability to understand the emotional landscape in communications and relationships and to respond appropriately. This assessment can be accessed online, and training can follow.

Let's see, how about **internships**? Effective candidates can use the time of dating and courting to gain skills in relationship development and management, not just swim in a sea of love hormones. (Disclosure: I did not take my own advice when I became engaged after mere weeks to Martin at the lovesick age of nineteen!)

And speaking of internships, my daughter, Claire, got more than her feet wet in family life experience as a nanny to multiple kids of multiple ages during her undergraduate studies at Wellesley College. She may have taken the work primarily for the extra cash, but the real life experience of keeping kids and learning to discipline and care for babies and toddlers led her to believe that the best incentive to use proper birth control is taking care of somebody else's children!

Looking at this job posting makes me realize how woefully underprepared I was to enter into the Business of Marriage. Thank goodness I was never fired, had some on-the-job training, and received a generous compensation in unconditional love. I'm glad I took the job.

Motivate the Team!

How to encourage the best
in every player on the family team.

*M*anagers understand that a key part of the job is motivating their staff to perform at the highest level. Great leaders and managers are considered great because they have an innate ability to inspire top performance in their employees. Coaches are often judged by how they motivate their teams. Teachers are evaluated by how they motivate their students. Ever thought of the role you play in motivating your family?

When was the last time you really thought about how you might motivate your significant other to reach his or her highest potential? Too often we major in the minors and get caught up in the routine at home—failing to practice the art of motivation while focusing on criticism or just plain inattention.

In a *Newsweek* commentary on the characteristics of winning teams, Jack and Suzy Welch wrote that attaining the highest performance from the team requires relentless coaching of middling performers and constant praise and reinforcement of star performers. I really like this concept for families. (The Welches also advocated that the best thing the leader could do for chronic underachievers is help them find the door; this strikes me as a poor practice for families!)

Let's look at the coaching aspect of this advice first. If there is one thing my husband and I have learned through business ownership, it is that we can't always just do it ourselves. We've learned we can take all kinds of time and resources teasing out how to improve our performance in some area—or we can bring in a great coach with the resources and experience to train us more efficiently.

We've brought that concept to the home front as well. A couple of years ago, Martin was suffering from "multi-task-ism." You know that disorder. You have lost all ability to focus because you have been subject to constant interruption from multiple sources. While this was affecting his work life, it was really creating issues at home where he always seemed to need to work rather than rest. He was distracted and unable to be fully present for our family.

I encouraged him to seek some mindfulness activity and he chose to take the six-week Mindfulness Based Stress Reduction course pioneered by Jon Kabat Zin. That course was almost immediately helpful. And when he felt himself slipping, he went right back for a refresher course.

I find that physical training helps motivate me and provides balance in my life. When I'm training for a marathon or half marathon, I perform better in many aspects of my life. I sleep better, eat better, have more energy, feel better about my body. I'm just plain happier. My husband has been a major source of support and coaching, riding along beside me on long runs, training with me for shorter races. And generally encouraging me to keep on keeping on.

Coaching or training in the form of counseling can save marriages. David Finch, the author of *The Journal of Best Practices: A Memoir of Marriage, Asperger Syndrome, and One Man's Quest to be a Better Husband*, literally trained himself to be the very best husband and father he could be by using notes—written on napkins and the backs of envelopes—as reminders to behave in ways that were better for him and his family. He wrote things like: "Don't change the radio station when Kristen's singing along." "Let Kristen shower in the morning without crowding her." "Give the kids vitamins without asking Kristen a million steps and directions on how to do that." He took seriously the need to train himself to be the best he could be at home. According to his website "guided by the journal of best practices, David transforms himself over the course of two years from the world's most trying husband to the husband who tries the hardest." It saved his marriage.

Now let's talk about positive feedback and encouragement. Encouraging and praising kids is often so easy. It can just roll out of you as you are charmed by your child's mastery of new skills or discovery of a hidden talent. But what about encouraging our spouse? Do you consciously try to encourage or praise your significant other daily? I think this one might be a bit harder for couples to practice. And I'm not sure why. Truth is, I've trained myself to pass along positive feedback from clients to our work team. I'm always conscious of the need my staff has to hear my praise. It's really just another training opportunity at home. We need to bring that level of consciousness to our spouses and to our families at home.

My husband doesn't know this, but when I consciously praise his efforts, he beams like a little boy! It's so endearing, and I can see the light in his eyes. He deserves much more of that feedback from me. And so does *your* significant other. All of us flourish when we know there is someone in our life who is behind us encouraging us to do our best. And that sort of communication has a reciprocal benefit—it leaves the giver of the feedback feeling just about as great as the receiver; a virtuous cycle indeed. Motivating others is motivating! So let's bring those good vibes home!

Call in the Consultants

A good consultant may be
just what your marriage needs.

*O*ver the years, my firm has used consultants very selectively and with great consideration. For the most part, these professionals have given us insights that have proven quite beneficial, although their true benefit to us has been in direct proportion to our willingness to follow their counsel and trust in their advice. Nonetheless, as I reflect on their guidance I believe they have been worth their sometimes high fees because they nudged shifts in our perception of "the right way" to run our business or manage our team that have created real and lasting change. This sort of change doesn't always happen as a result of attending a conference or workshop. And as much as I have learned and felt influenced by reading books or taking online courses, it can take a relationship and an engagement over time to truly embody the lessons taught in these resources.

I've been thinking about marriage and specifically the number of partners who are intimidated or are unwilling to use professional counseling to improve their marriages. Like it or not, there is still a stigma toward reaching out to a counselor to help in marriage as though this is an admission that there is a problem or that the marriage isn't perfect—maybe even at risk. I find this sad because consultants are brought into businesses to solve hard problems, improve lower-than-wanted results, and even save a sinking business, and no one would call this move a sign of weakness. Instead we see it as a mark of wisdom.

Consultants are called into a business for several reasons. First, we use them when we are stuck in a problem or pattern and want an objective viewpoint to help us get "unstuck." Martin and I used consultants in this way to spur sales growth when we found ourselves in a year-over-year pattern of stasis. Consultants have the advantage of objectivity. They can come into an organization, study its processes and patterns, and make a clearer assessment of the gap that is keeping the organization from moving forward. Maybe the organization is not applying enough human or capital resources. Perhaps it needs better training or even a more conscious process-driven approach.

Martin likes to tell our clients that trying to discern your own brand is like trying to pull your own teeth—it's possible, but often bloody and painful. An objective eye can be so valuable in seeing that forest beyond the trees and helping us find the path out of the woods.

Couples often find themselves in the forest with no clear way out. And, like the business consultant, a good counselor can help a couple who has found themselves stuck in a pattern of anger and conflict. (If you live together long enough, you will find yourself there.) This ability to see the situation objectively and provide perspective, better skills, and a way out of the cycle of drama releases tremendous healing and energy back into the relationship.

I have a dear friend who belongs to a different denomination from her husband. Both are deeply religious, and early in their marriage, as they were raising their family, they became stuck in a disagreement about which faith to raise their children in. They were experiencing deep stress, and it was eroding their marital team spirit. I suggested a counselor whom I respected and trusted, and in a few meetings, they were able to agree and work out a plan to present their children with experience and understanding of both denominations and then let each of them choose their own path. They moved from feeling defeated by these differences in their belief systems to celebrating the rich faith understanding that living in a household with two faith viewpoints allowed. And it must have worked, because one of their children is a minister and another has gone into church work.

Consultants provide expertise that doesn't currently reside in the business. Martin and I are often called in as consultants in this way. The marketing department and sales team have a deep bench of professionals, but few organizations keep on staff a brand leadership and marketing integration specialist. These are skills that are just a bit different from those required on a daily basis, and they have been honed over a thirty-five-year work history. So our firm can be very valuable in teaching our clients how to use brand behavior to lead an organization internally and communicate and market the brand externally.

While I understand there are graduate programs in family studies, I don't know a single person with an advanced degree in marital and family relations. Do you? I don't recall many classes on the art of raising a child. There aren't even many classes on basic family finances. So how are we to know the best and most effective skills for managing marital conflict or creating the best possible marital relationship? Most of us just bring the tools we learned from our family into our roles as mate or parent; and unless our parents were absolute experts, we probably have some skills that could stand improvement. Shouldn't we engage some professional consulting to help us achieve the relationship we want?

Martin and I have made excellent use of a counselor to learn better ways of communicating with each other. The counselor challenged our current skill set and the deep-seated beliefs that lay behind them so that we could behave in ways that were more productive and generated intimacy and trust. And if we're being really honest, we'd be real about the level of sexual education we all have, especially as it relates to long-term monogamy, and realize the value of getting help in this arena if we need it.

Often consultants are brought in to manage a big organizational change. Change management is really difficult; humans are a big bundle of habits, and we just wobble and wobble in the face of change no matter how good the outcome might be. Learning to change is an art, and it takes skilled professionals to support us as we move through big changes in business and in life.

Not long ago I was diagnosed with a serious disease; I had no words to describe what I was feeling as I was faced with a life that was going to look nothing like I had envisioned. I needed to make changes in order to optimize my health and fight for my life and myself. I needed to understand what was happening to me and adjust to this new normal. And I needed to assess where I was in my personal journey and course-correct where needed so that I could live the vibrant, happy life I so wanted.

There was no way my hematologist could do all that for me. I needed a consulting team. And so I put together a team of medical doctors, alternative medicine practitioners, counselors, and advisors. Together, we've been marching through the process of change and adaptation. I can't lead my life now with the prior level of naïveté or disregard for the fleeting quality of life that I had before. My consulting team keeps me on the track to health, happiness, and gratitude for this beautiful, fragile life.

Finally, the big dogs are called in when a business is in a downhill slide toward failure and the organization needs a life-boat and a way to surface and settle. When we're slowly going under and we have lost our breath, we simply can't save our-selves; we need that hand to pull us back up. This is a time when the decision should not be *whether* to call in a consultant but rather *how soon* we can make our way to a good one. I wonder how many marriages would have survived if couples could understand that they can't really expect to go it alone and work things out when they are in this deepest of relationship wells. And if in the end the marriage needs to dissolve, then a counselor can help to ease the path of separation and dissolution immea-surably. No business would think about dissolving without excel-lent legal and financial guidance. Why do we pretend we don't need help during these toughest of personal situations?

Finally, a word of advice from one who has some experience here. We can sit in a therapist's office and talk until we're blue in the face. It is interesting, it can make us feel good and even fool us into believing we're getting something done. But the true benefit of any consulting gig comes from setting aside our habits, beliefs, and patterns of behavior, and truly doing the work. That means trying the things our counselors ask us to do no matter how weird or silly they may seem. Then changing our behaviors and creating new habits based on these new experiences—and deriving real benefit from the change or new skills our consult-ants are seeking to help us with. You can sit in a counselor's office and talk, then walk right out and be the same old person, saying and doing the same old things; or you can stretch, try, and grow into a better mate with better habits and better skills. But you have work to do, and no one else can do that for you.

When Martin and I consult, we don't do the work, we facilitate the work. Do *your* work to achieve success.

As I write this book, I am clear on the role I wish to play in the lives of my readers. I am not a marital counselor; I do not hold a degree in psychology or social work. I am your friend. I offer my insights as one who has made the journey for forty years and who has been helped by my unique insight into the parallels of being in business and being in marriage with Martin. And I offer thoughts and ideas as enhancements and conversation starters to you and your mate. But I'm not the consultant here, and I sincerely hope that you will make good use of counselors to consult you along the journey when you find you need an objective eye or a new skill. And when change and hardship come, as they inevitably do, I hope that you will find dignity and pride in seeking help and receive the support and healing that you need.

About the Author

Melissa Thoma is co-founder and principal with Little Rock, Arkansas-based brand strategy and marketing communications firm Thoma Thoma. Since starting the firm in 1988, Melissa has worn many hats as an entrepreneur: business leader, speech and presentation coach, human resource manager, creative director and brand strategist.

Melissa created a special practice area focused on marketing to women, wrote a regular column titled "The Business of Marriage" for WomenEntrepreneur.com, and led development of numerous agency consultative services, including The Brand Navigator™, The Creativity Catalyst™, The Media Coach™ and The Presentation Coach™. Today she provides senior strategic counsel to both clients and agency personnel.

A staunch supporter of the arts, Melissa is a bit of a renaissance woman, having been known to perform opera and musical theatre, sing bluegrass in the family band, run marathons, teach cooking and wine appreciation classes, indulge in more than one book club, enjoy vegan cookery and occasionally binge on reality TV.

She is most proud of her forty-year marriage, her two smart, successful, loving children and their families, and the sweet, sweet moments she's shared with a tribe of extended family and friends.

www.ingramcontent.com/pod-product-compliance
Lightning Source LLC
LaVergne TN
LVHW010315070426
835509LV00029B/3498